HAPPY DAYS

Jenny Scott

HAPPY DAYS

Jenny Scott

The story of the Methodist community in the
Lincolnshire village of Saxilby

Cirencester

Mereo Books

2nd Floor, 6-8 Dyer Street, Cirencester, Gloucestershire, GL7 2PF
An imprint of Memoirs Books. www.mereobooks.com
and www.memoirsbooks.co.uk

Happy Days

First published in Great Britain in 2022
by Mereo Books, an imprint of Memoirs Books.

ISBN: 978-1-86151-868-2

The address for Memoirs Books can be
found at www.mereobooks.com

Mereo Books Ltd. Reg. No. 12157152

Typeset in 11/18pt Aktiv Grotesk
by Wiltshire Associates.
Printed and bound in Great Britain

This book is dedicated to all the people who have had connections with Saxilby Chapel over the years, as well as the generations who have gone before

A special dedication to my wonderful husband Ray, without whom this book could never have been written, for his constant help and support.

Finally, a big thank you to our granddaughter Madeleine for designing the front cover, which really does convey the 'Happy Days' shared by so many over the years

Contents

Foreword

Introduction

Foreword

Saxilby and District History Group was formed in 2000 with the intention of gathering memories of our community. It soon became evident from the amount of material we received that we had enough to publish a book on the history of our ancient village. The book, 'Step Back in Time', was published in 2005. It has been followed by a further book, 'Saxilby Past and Present – a Century of Change'.

Jenny, together with her husband Ray, have been active members of the History Group for several years. Since Jenny has lived in the village all her life, her depth of local knowledge (and excellent memory) have been invaluable in helping to research the history of the district.

This book is a welcome addition to the history of Saxilby. It adds not only to our local history, but also to the social history of the county in general and the history of the growth and development of the Methodist movement. Indeed the fortunes of Methodism can be seen in the history of Saxilby itself, from public meetings in the early 1800s and the building of the first chapel in 1808 to the closure of the last chapel just two years ago.

The Methodist movement has its roots on the Isle of Axholme; I myself, like the father of Methodism, John Wesley, am proud to call myself a 'Yellowbelly'!

Chris Hewis
Chairman
Saxilby and District History Group
March 2022

Introduction

The decision to close Saxilby Methodist Church during 2020 had already taken place, but the pandemic put a stop to the carefully planned programme of events which would have enabled people to come together and say farewell over a period of months, which left members feeling quite bereft. The idea of writing a book telling the story of Methodism in Saxilby began when the chapel was finally sold in March 2021, and is dedicated to all the people who have had connections with Saxilby Chapel over the years, as well as the generations who have gone before.

My own family have been involved with local Methodism throughout its 200+ year history. Indeed someone recently described me as a 'child of the chapel', as my formative years were spent within the large family that made up the Godfrey Memorial Chapel during the 1950s-60s, so personal photos and recollections made a good starting point. It soon became apparent that in order to try to understand the rather complicated history of Methodism in Saxilby, it would make sense to start at the very beginning, explaining how the movement began, the courage of the early members who dared to rebel against the rituals of the established church and how it impacted on the community. Through my research, wonderful stories have been discovered of people who influenced the movement, showing how their commitment to the chapel and wider community helped bring about social change in our corner of Lincolnshire. Local people may recognise names and events from the past, but I hope other readers just enjoy reading the history of the movement and how a small Lincolnshire village came to have three different chapels, all flourishing for over 80 years, before finally uniting once more and building the new chapel in 1940.

Methodism has always been community based, each chapel providing a way of showing the love of God in action, giving people the opportunity to experience personal forgiveness, love and renewal, and empowering them to go out and help those less fortunate. In the early years there was educational support, where individuals were encouraged to realise their own talents, gaining confidence to use their abilities both within the chapel and the community. The 'chapel family' has always been wide and all-encompassing, a sentiment which has remained true throughout the years. Everyone is welcome, yet we ae constantly looking beyond our own congregation, caring for those in need in this country and across the world.

Throughout the book runs a constant theme of change, beginning with the breakaway groups within Methodism itself, which led to Saxilby having three separate chapels, all coming from John Wesley's original movement, but striving to make worship meaningful in their own individual, independent ways. Added to which are changes within society during the years, from state education, industrialisation and the coming of the railway to the recent innovations and opportunities of modern technology that would have seemed unbelievable 200 years ago. Alongside all this has been the cultural change in people's freedom to choose their own path, rather than accepting the traditions of the past and whilst the ideals of Methodism have kept constant, giving families a sense of inclusion and a refuge in times of conflict, it becomes apparent that perhaps the structure of the movement has not kept pace with the fast-changing world we live in today.

The gradual closures of small chapels throughout the 1950s-70s have now become all too frequent, not just in Lincolnshire but across the country, and whilst Saxilby Chapel has done incredible work and tried its hardest to adapt and change in order to remain relevant to the community it serves, eventually it too had to take the painful decision to close.

You will notice that I've used the world 'chapel' throughout the book, although the word itself relates to the building, which became conflated with the Methodist Church, meaning the society that worships there. However, in order to differentiate between the Anglicans and Methodists, many communities, including the village of Saxilby, have always used 'chapel' to mean the Methodist Church. The term hasn't been in general use for many years, but in order not to confuse readers, I've stayed with the word 'chapel' throughout the book, so apologies to the generations who are no longer familiar with the terminology.

To all the people who have taken on the many roles within the chapel, working tirelessly over the years to keep Methodism alive and flourishing, this book is a way of saying thank you for your dedication and commitment. Thanks also to members, past and present, who have shared their memories with me, especially Gill Pacey, who has provided so much detail about the early years. It's been very special to remember happy times in this period of uncertainty. Whilst trying to ensure the book provides an accurate history of the chapel, there will doubtless be errors, omissions or events that are in the wrong time-frame, and for that I can only apologise, especially as the later chapters have been written without access to recent minute books and registers.

As a reference guide, a list of the key dates and a timetable of all the Ministers and their families who looked after the congregation at the Godfrey Memorial Methodist Church is given at the back of the book.

Finally a word about the title, which has come from a phrase used by everyone I've spoken to. Without exception all have talked about the happiness they enjoyed at the chapel, so I hope you enjoy reading *Happy Days*, the Story of the Methodist community in the Lincolnshire Village of Saxilby.

Chapter 1

1703–1807: The Beginning of Methodism

In order to understand the popularity of Methodism, why it appealed so much to ordinary people up and down the country and the impact on the villagers in Saxilby, let's begin with the history of the movement, where the name came from and how it developed during those early years, especially as it was the various reforms which took place that led to Saxilby having three different chapels.

John Wesley was the founder of the Methodist movement. He was born in 1703 and brought up in the Lincolnshire village of Epworth, where his father was a rector in the Anglican church. There were 19 children in the family (although only nine survived infancy) and all were taught at home by their mother, who was a strict disciplinarian. Life was rigidly structured and the children learned to be quiet, obedient and hardworking. When John was just five years old, the rectory burned down and everyone rushed to leave the burning building, but in the confusion John was left inside. Fortunately he woke up and managed to open a window and was rescued, just as the blazing roof of the house fell in. His mother always believed he had been spared by God for important work.

John studied at Oxford University, gaining a Master's degree in 1727, and after spending a year assisting his father in Epworth, became an ordained priest in the Church of England. He then returned to Oxford and joined the society his younger brother Charles had founded, known as 'The Holy Club', whose members were devoted to prayer, taking communion regularly, spending time every day studying the scriptures, and going out visiting the sick and the poor, as well as those in prison. When John took over, he established structures as to how the group should operate, what time they should devote to study and when they should go out visiting. Because the members were so 'methodical' in everything they did, many students gave them the rather satirical nick-name 'Methodist' and the name became established.

On leaving Oxford, John and his brother Charles were invited to visit the American colony of Georgia to oversee the spiritual lives of the people. It was on the crossing that they first came into contact with some Moravian settlers, who displayed great faith and spirituality during a violent storm, which made a lasting impression on them both. Unfortunately the mission in Georgia did not work out well, as the congregation refused to adhere to the rules and disciplines of the 'Holy Club' which the brothers tried to enforce, so they returned to London feeling rather disheartened.

John then met another Moravian Christian named Peter Boehler, who persuaded him to have more faith. Rather reluctantly, John went along to a society meeting in Aldersgate Street, London, where he experienced what he called his 'evangelical conversion' when he felt his heart strangely warmed during a reading of Martin Luther's preface to the Epistle to the Romans. This was the moment that John realised that faith in Christ could indeed overcome everything, and that by praising God and asking forgiveness, His love would show compassion and mercy to all who repented.

From this point onward, at the age of 35, John viewed his mission in life as one of proclaiming the good news of redemption by faith and joined a former member of the 'Holy Club' George Whitefield, who was having remarkable success as a preacher in Bristol. George was preaching outdoors to the working-class poor, oppressed by industrialisation and neglected by the established church. To begin with John felt uncomfortable with this outdoor style of preaching, far removed from the established worship he was used to in the Church of England, but he soon realised that he was reaching the very people he wanted to help.

With his organisational skills John quickly became the new leader of the movement, which became known as Methodism, preaching the message that everyone can be saved and no one is beyond the reach of God's love. The Church of England did not approve of this new type of preaching, seeing it as a social threat, disregarding the traditions of the establishment. They began to attack the movement, meetings were disrupted and John soon found he was no longer welcome to preach in Anglican Church services. People who turned to Methodism became known as 'dissenters' (from the Latin *dissentire* 'to disagree'), rebelling against the established church which was failing them and being brave enough to accept this new way of worship. John took courage from this, as he truly believed he had been called by God to save the people that the church, which had become out of touch with their congregations, was failing. Nothing would stand in his way to stop him delivering this message.

So he took to travelling around the country on horseback, preaching outdoors and forming small Christian groups who would meet together in what became known as societies (we might call them groups or clubs) for the nurture of the Christian faith and way of life. The meetings were always full of passion and enthusiasm, which can be captured by John Wesley's famous 'Rule of Life' quote: 'Do all the good you can, by all the means you can, in all the ways you can, in all the places you can, at all the times you can, to all the people you can, as long as ever you can.'

When these societies became too large for members to care for each other, a 'class system' was introduced. Each class would have twelve members with one person designated as the leader, meeting weekly to pray, read the bible and to talk to each other about their faith and how they were living their lives. In order to continue to provide spiritual guidance to these societies, John approved 'lay preachers', local people who were not ordained by the Anglican Church, but who could be trained to preach to the people each Sunday, with John visiting each society regularly, in what became known as the quarterly visit. In 1771 he made the decision that women as well as men should be allowed to preach, which was quite radical. Lay people would also play a major part in the running of their local church where, as well as taking services, people would be appointed 'stewards' to take responsibility for the fabric of the church buildings, counting collections and looking after the day-to-day running of the society.

People who attended meetings regularly and who were committed to the beliefs of Methodism became *members*, a similar concept to confirmation in the Anglican faith. If the person had not been baptised, then the service of membership would include baptism, indeed making a commitment to the Methodist Church is still called 'membership' today. However, you didn't have to be a member to attend Methodist services, so the number of people attending meetings was always much greater than the number of committed members.

As the number of societies increased, John simply could not visit them all himself, so he drew up a set of 'general rules' for each society, laying the foundations of the Methodist Church Connexion, meaning the whole movement would act and make decisions together. At local levels the societies were grouped into circuits, to which travelling preachers were appointed for three year terms, which is where the term 'itinerant' comes from. Circuit officials would meet quarterly under a senior travelling preacher, with Wesley presiding over an annual conference to co-ordinate doctrine and discipline for the whole connexion.

The societies needed places to worship in, so barns, outbuildings or rooms in houses were used, and these became known as 'chapels' or 'meeting houses'. As soon as the congregation was able to move to a proper building, it was a mark of progress and the larger accommodation gave the society a sense of status and respectability. The buildings were looked after by a body of people called 'trustees', who would safeguard the chapels in line with Methodist purposes.

Charles Wesley supported his brother in the growing movement and being a highly gifted musician and poet he had already started to write hymns, taking religious texts as well the everyday trials people were experiencing and setting them to music. The rousing tunes and messages of faith and hope of these hymns became a source of inspiration to people and were instrumental in spreading the Methodist movement as people could sing them throughout the week, not just on a Sunday. His first selection of hymns was published in 1739 and before he died he had written over six thousand hymns, leading to a familiar saying: 'Methodism was born in song'.

With John returning regularly to his Lincolnshire home village of Epworth, he made several journeys along the Trent Valley over the years, and would often stop at villages along the way and preach to the rural communities, setting up small societies. Newton-on-Trent had a society in existence before the year 1750 and John himself came to preach on four occasions between 1770 and 1786, his diary describing his first visit: *'We rode through heavy rain to Newton upon Trent. The weather was clearing up, I preached before the house to an earnest congregation. A people more loving, more artless or more athirst for God, I have seldom seen.'* The early meetings were held at the home of Caroline Skelton with a chapel being built around 1795, followed by a new chapel which was in use from 1895 to 2011.

Despite his regular visits to Epworth, John didn't come to the city of Lincoln itself until the year 1780. By this time he was 76 years of age and had been speaking in Newark when he received a request from a resident of Lincoln to go and preach in the city, so, travelling on horseback as usual, he made the journey to Lincoln. He used the services of the town crier to announce his visit, and at 6 o'clock in the evening of the 30th June 1780, he found himself addressing a large crowd at the top of Castle Hill, where he preached on 'The Word of Life'. A book by George Barratt, published in 1866, goes on to describe what happened the following day when he preached again in the open air at 10 o'clock in the morning:

About half-way through the sermon, a violent storm arose, and as the rain poured down, the keeper of the court-house opened the door and allowed the preacher and the entire congregation to enter the building, with Mr Wesley taking his stand where the magistrates usually sat to administer justice, proceeded in preaching the Gospel of God.

Although John visited Lincoln several times after his initial visit and was supported by a few individuals in the city who became Methodists, there was so much opposition from the established church that it was a number of years before a society started in Lincoln. It took a lady called Sarah Parrot from Sturton, who walked twenty-seven miles to Gonerby near Grantham, to appeal to a devout lady with financial means called Mrs Fisher to move to the City and open a place of worship. The society first met in 1787 using an old lumber room near Gowts Bridge with just four ladies gathered together, but as Mrs Fisher already knew various preachers, she invited them to Lincoln to help build the numbers. Before long they moved to new premises on the south side of the river, opposite the Ship Inn, with John returning to preach there. He was described as 'more like an angel than a man' with his long silvery hair, parted in the middle.

John Wesley, 'with his long silvery hair parted in the middle'

By 1815 the number of Methodists in the city warranted the building of a more convenient and sizable establishment, so a new chapel was erected in Bank Street. One of the preachers at the opening service was Richard Watson, a joiner at the time, who had heard John Wesley speak when he first visited Lincoln, and who attracted the crowds with his 'sweetly flowing eloquence'. Mr Watson went on to become President of the Conference and Secretary of the Missionary Society. The more societies there were however, the louder the critics became, with meetings often being broken up with violence, and the wider the division between the Methodist Movement and the Church of England became, but John steadfastly remained an Anglican until he died in March 1791 at the age of 87.

From such small beginnings in the Lincolnshire village of Epworth, John Wesley's influence has reached every corner of the globe, with an estimated 70 million Methodists in the world today, a lasting legacy from such a great preacher. In his biography, Stephen Tomkins wrote: 'During his life John Wesley rode 250,000 miles, gave away £30,000 and preached more than 40,000 sermons. He spoke out against the slave trade and by the time of his death he had 135,00 members and 541 itinerant preachers under the name Methodist.'

John Wesley never intended to start a separate church; indeed he encouraged all his congregations to continue to attend their Parish Church, making sure meetings of his 'Methodist Societies' should never clash with the services of Church of England. He also maintained that the church which took his name, 'Wesleyan Methodism', should follow the path of the established church by allowing only ordained ministers to take Sacrament and to conduct baptisms, marriages and funerals. The movement should also follow the rules he had set out, which governed how the Connexion operated.

When he was in his 80s, John set up a structure called 'The Yearly Conference of the People called Methodists' in order to ensure the continuation of the movement after his death. Within four years of John's death the body of people in charge of the Conference decided to go against his wishes, allowing Methodist preachers to become legally entitled to conduct marriages and administer the sacraments, meaning Methodism becoming completely separate from the Church of England. The Conference also began making new rules and regulations regarding the governance of each chapel, which according to William Leary's book "Lincolnshire Methodism", made the ruling body seem high-handed and dominating to many local congregations, who were used to running their own chapels, and within a few years various reform movements began breaking away from the Wesleyans and different branches of Methodism were formed.

The largest breakaway movement happened In 1807, only 16 years after John Wesley's death, when two lay preachers called Hugh Bourne and William Clowes formed a group known as the 'Primitive Methodists'. The word primitive of course means 'simple' or 'relating to an original stage' and this was exactly what this movement wanted, to return to the earlier form of Methodism that Wesley had started, reaching out to the poor and marginalised in a down-to-earth way. They had no prayer book and relied heavily on lay preachers, rather than being dominated by central authority, ensuring that it was the members at circuit level who should take decisions about how their movement evolved. This gave them much more freedom in their worship and they appealed to the rural poor and the working class. In other words, whilst Wesleyan Methodism was a church *for* the poor, Primitive Methodism was a church *of* the poor.

Both Hugh Bourne and William Clowes were charismatic

preachers and they organised 'camp meetings' which were events, held in the open air, involving virtually non-stop preaching, public praying and hymn singing late into the night, sometimes going on for two or three days. The idea originated on the American frontier and could lead to many emotional conversion experiences. They were sometimes nick-named 'Ranters', as the preachers would rant without stopping for some considerable time. Such meetings were a regular feature of Primitive Methodist life and still survive today, with meetings held at large sites where large crowds gather and experience a collective revival of faith. Primitives liked to keep everything simple, their chapels and type of worship reflecting this, keeping their language simple, even dressing plainly, focusing their efforts on reaching out to the working class and educating them.

Meanwhile as the Wesleyan Methodists strived to become respectable and accepted as a reputable church, there followed more breakaway movements, none as large as the Primitive Methodists, but all wanting a more democratic form of church governance. There was the formation of the New Methodist Connexion, the Protestant Methodists and the Wesleyan Association, but the greatest upheaval occurred in 1849 and began with what one historian called 'the paper war', which eventually led to the creation of the Wesleyan Reform Society, before it became the United Methodist Free Church in 1857.

For several years, three ministers, James Everett, William Griffith and Samuel Dunn, had been lobbying for reform, but the break finally came when leaflets and pamphlets of 'The Wesley Banner' were distributed anonymously.

Conference removed the three ministers deemed responsible, which caused massive upheaval. Local ministers and lay-members all became involved as the Connexion charged everyone who supported any type of reform with disloyalty. This in turn led to protests against the way the expulsions had occurred and reactions against those who tried to suppress the lay-people supporting the reformers. The movement escalated and soon hundreds of people were expelled for attending any meetings led by the reformers, which were happening up and down the country.

The three ministers who had been expelled were all great speakers and willingly travelled round the circuits by invitation, giving encouragement to any congregations who wanted reform. James Everett came to this part of Lincolnshire and addressed a crowded meeting in Lincoln Corn Exchange, followed by another enthusiastic meeting in Gainsborough. News from these meetings spread to the villages where local congregations liked the idea of reform and new places of worship were hastily found to house the growing number of reformers. In Lincolnshire the figures mirrored the national picture with a loss of about a quarter of the membership from the Wesleyan Church but in Saxilby there was an exodus of about 60% who moved to the Reformer movement.

You might be thinking what a radical group Methodists were, challenging and rebelling, but this is what the movement evoked: free thinkers, people who weren't afraid to act on their beliefs but with a strong sense of duty. Yet throughout all the splits and reforms, everyone still held fast to their faith that Methodism had inspired, following a similar pattern of worship that John Wesley had promoted, but refusing to accept the same rules of how local societies should operate. No wonder it held real appeal to ordinary people, across all social classes, Methodism offered a sense of self-determination, with services overflowing with inspiration and enthusiasm, as well as sharing the faith, hope and love with everyone, no matter what their circumstances might be.

Chapter 2

1808-1839: Methodism arrives in Saxilby

Picture what life in a village like Saxilby would be like in the early 1800s. There would have been no transport, other than a horse and cart, the nearest town being some six miles away, which would have been an arduous journey on foot. The only employment for most people would be on a local farm, becoming a domestic servant or joining a village business such as a butcher, blacksmith, carpenter or grocer. Life for most of the community would be basic, with lighting by lamp or candle and no running water. The 'privy' would be outside, and only the children of the more affluent few would receive any sort of education. You begin to understand just how remote small settlements would be and how isolated the villages were from what was going on in the wider world.

Indeed, two tiny neighbouring villages received Methodism almost 30 years before it arrived in Saxilby. George Barrett's book *Recollections of Methodism in the City of Lincoln* tells us that societies existed around 1780 in both Broxholme and Sturton, but no record exists to show the numbers of members. What we do know is that 'Mr William Mawer from Broxholme and Mr Wm Flintham from Sturton became local preachers. They are both described in George Barrett's book as men of sound judgment, knowledge of the Gospel and the ability to teach its doctrines, and with William Mawer being called a poetic genius'. They obviously didn't preach their message in Saxilby however, because it wasn't until 1808 that Methodism finally arrived in the village when a young dynamic speaker called Thomas Jackson came to bring news of the movement. He was a self-taught son of an agricultural labourer, but he became a preacher on the Spilsby circuit at the age of 21 before moving to Lincoln.

It would have been quite an event in the rather humdrum existence of village life to have someone different coming to speak about a new way of living, so I'm sure he would have attracted attention. Plus we know from history that Thomas was a renowned preacher, speaking to people in a way they would have understood and conveying the message that God loved everyone; no matter who you were, rich or poor, educated or not, if you had faith and believed, then life could be transformed. As you read the account of what took place, try to visualise the village high street as it would have been then, only a small number of properties on one side of the street and just open fields and scrub land on the other. The premises which is now the funeral home were already occupied by the Rook family, who ran a grocery shop, and as they became Methodists, I've envisaged that this event possibly took place somewhere nearby on the High Street.

The full account of Thomas Jackson's visit to Saxilby is best reported by this passage he wrote in his journal:

In the year 1808, accompanied by a zealous friend, I went, on a cold day in March, to Saxilby, where the voice of no Methodist Preacher had been previously heard.

My companion went from house to house informing the people that a young man would deliver a sermon in the open air; a shopkeeper lent me an empty tea-chest to stand upon.

A considerable number of people attended, and formed a large semicircle, but not one of them would venture to come very near me. But, by lifting up my voice, I succeeded in making them hear; and not in vain. This beginning was followed up by others; regular preaching was introduced, and a Society formed.

Soon, as Thomas Jackson recounted, other travelling preachers came to the village and a Wesleyan Methodist Society began in Saxilby during 1808, their first chapel being a building close to the High Street, at the rear of the building which used to be The Masons Arms, the driveway still being called 'Chapel Yard' today.

Photograph of the original Methodist Chapel taken during the 1980s

In the book *A History of Methodism in the Neighbourhood and City of Lincoln*, Mr A Watmough recorded that in 1811 there were 25 members in the Saxilby society, but remember only those committed to the movement would be accepted as members and the actual number of people in the congregations would have been a great deal larger. Methodism was something which was completely radical at this time, appealing to the individual with a message of faith, hope and love, but it would have been a bold move to join the movement. Yet many people did, right across the social spectrum, and over the next 25 years the number of members in the village increased. We know from early records that William Conyers, a local bricklayer, was listed as being a steward in this era and he continued as a local preacher in the area for many years.

My own maternal family, who had lived in Saxilby since the mid-1700s, became members of the Methodist church in these early years. The family name was Keyworth and father John was a local butcher, and all their family became Methodists and worshipped in the village for 200 years. John had two sons with his second wife Mary, John and Richard, who married two sisters, Rebekah and Anne Wilkinson from Thorpe on the Hill, where there had been a Methodist society since 1797. Richard married Anne and became a farmer on Saxilby Moor, whilst John, being the eldest, followed in his father's footsteps and became a butcher and married Rebekah. Together they had a large family with many of them holding roles within the Methodist community:

Martin, born 1811, was John and Rebecca's eldest son. He married a miller's daughter, Sarah Howard, and built the mill down Broadholme Lane in Saxilby, on land adjoining his Uncle Richard's farm on Saxilby Moor (Gainsborough Road). They had seven children, who were all educated initially at home, even the females of the family, which in those days was quite unusual. He was also my great-great-grandfather. Martin was highly respected in the neighbourhood and attended the Methodist Chapel, where he was much loved as a Sunday School teacher; his obituary reported him often being surrounded by about 150 children! He was a trustee of Hardwick chapel when it opened, helping ensure the message was carried to every village, however small.

Broadholme Mill, home of Martin Keyworth & Family

Daughter Mary, born 1814, married William Hardy, a local carpenter, who attended the chapel with his parents John and Mary. Both William and his father John were trustees of Hardwick Chapel. Mary and William had five daughters before their son William was born in 1851 and he, in turn, became a steward at the Wesley Chapel in 1883 and was much involved in the extensive alterations which took place in 1885.

The next son, Robert, was born in 1816, and he made Methodism his life by becoming a Wesleyan Minister. By the time the Centenary chapel opened in 1839, he was already a Methodist Minister in training and had left Saxilby to pursue his profession. Thereafter he moved around the country regularly as, of course, he could only be minister in one place for three or four years at that time. He went on to have a son named John Wesley Keyworth, who also became a Wesleyan Methodist Minister.

It was the third son, William born in 1821, who went into his father's business and became a butcher. He married Sarah Simms, from Glentworth, and had a very large family, who all worshipped at the chapel.

Their youngest son, Ira, was a talented musician and there is still a manuscript book containing his beautiful handwritten compositions, which were all on religious themes.

John Wesley's structures for how societies should work ensured that everyone within the Methodist family was valued and encouraged and this had huge appeal within the community, as it promoted a sense of belonging. The class meetings would be taking place each week, when 12 people would come together under the leadership of one member and often the 'class leaders' would be the more affluent and educated in the society, doing all they could to empower their fellow members. Remember one of the key features of Methodism means being filled with the love of God and to show that love to other people throughout their lives, committed to helping those less fortunate. There would also be help for those with little or no education, teaching them to read and write, giving them confidence as they became used to speaking aloud to others.

Sunday services were hugely popular because there was freedom to worship in a way people understood and felt was relevant to their lives. Sermons were given by lay preachers the congregation could identify with, being inspired and encouraged by the message of compassion for all, no matter who they were or what they did. Hymns were accompanied by members playing fiddles or other musical instruments, which meant members always enjoyed a 'good sing'. Indeed the singing became the heart of the 'feel-good factor' that people felt at the chapel, as we all know how music really can lift the soul and Methodist services always did that.

All around the county more and more people were turning to Methodism, with Lincoln building an imposing chapel in 1836 known as 'Big Wesley', so called because it could seat a congregation of one thousand people. In Saxilby it became obvious that a much larger chapel was needed and in 1839 the society secured a site on the High Street, where the car sales forecourt now stands. It was named the Wesley Centenary Church as it marked the occasion of John Wesley's conversion in 1739 and was the home of Methodism in Saxilby until the other chapels opened in the middle of the century.

The Wesley Centenary Chapel, Saxilby, built in 1839

It might be worth mentioning here just how life at this time was defined by the structure of social class in the country, whether in towns or villages, as well as the effects of being rich or poor. Suddenly here was a religion which appealed across all sections of society and whilst there might still be an inbuilt respect between the classes, the ethos of the Methodism movement meant that those who had money would offer financial help in a variety of different ways to assist with the growing membership and the many new converts. We see this playing out across the years, how the more affluent members would offer employment to chapel folk, use the services of the tradespeople who were Methodists, as well as ensuring the fabric of the church was well maintained.

Thomas Jackson, who had been the first person to bring Methodism to the village back in 1808, writes in his autobiography how he came to Saxilby some 40 years later and was pleased to see a chapel in the centre of the village:

'In passing through this village of late years by the railway, I have observed a respectable-looking Methodist Chapel in the midst of the population; indicating that the people are at present more familiar with the preaching which half a century ago they were willing to hear, but not without suspicion as to the preacher's intentions.'

Chapter 3

1840-1880: Saxilby's Three Chapels

By the middle of the 19th century the industrial revolution was sweeping across the country, changing the way people lived their lives in ways they could never have imagined, with schools starting, the railways arriving and factories opening up to manufacture products vital to the development of the country. Lincolnshire was regarded predominantly as an agricultural county, and as such the industrialisation was linked to farming. The first company in Lincoln was established by Nathaniel Clayton, who in 1842 formed a partnership with his brother-in-law, Joseph Shuttleworth, named 'Clayton Shuttleworth'. They built the first portable steam engine, quickly followed by a threshing machine.

Factories had a profound effect on education because

until now there had been no free schooling and it was left to Sunday Schools to provide basic reading and writing to the working class. As industry developed, the government began to realise that in order to make more money for the country, people needed to be educated, especially the young, and in 1833 the Factory Act was passed, making two hours of education a day compulsory for children working in factories.

The government also granted money to charities to help set up schools and in 1845 the Church of England authorities decided to build a school in Saxilby, at a cost of just over £400, known as Saxilby National Mixed School. During the first year it educated 151 scholars (89 boys and 62 girls) and whilst it wasn't completely free (boys had to pay 2d per week and girls paid 1d per week) these small fees did not make the school self-supporting, and the deficit had to be made up by subscriptions and other means. It was however incredibly popular and within the next few years it became necessary to enlarge the school in order to admit more pupils. In 1871 an infant school was built at a cost of £335, to accommodate 74 children up to the age of seven.

Up until this point of time Lincolnshire as a county had been virtually isolated except for access by the waterways, with the roads either poor or non-existent, but in 1846 the railway arrived in Lincoln and soon the whole county was covered with a criss-cross of train tracks, until most villages of any size had a service. The first railway in Saxilby was the branch line from Gainsborough to Lincoln, opened in 1848. It was followed by other train operators and soon trains were leaving or stopping at the village six or seven times a day. People connected with the railway moved into the village, needing places to live and sharing stories of life in other towns and communities, and for the first time there was an opportunity for ordinary working people to move around the county and beyond. By 1879 a station had been built, costing almost £1000, and a stationmaster was in post. Gradually new services began operating, linking up to stations with access to the main lines across the country, meaning goods could be carried with ease. More importantly, people could move about more freely and the community began to see an opening up of new opportunities.

New employment was emerging from all these changes, not just from work on the railways but from new types of business. Saxilby was lucky to be the place where the Lindsey & Kesteven Chemical Manure Company decided to establish its base, known locally as the 'chemical works', which opened in 1860. An early type of chemical manure involved the invention of superphosphate (the extraction of phosphorus from crushed bones treated with sulphuric acid) which could be used to enhance crops, but the transportation of the acid required in the manufacturing process was difficult, meaning it was easier to establish vitriol plants on site. A location beside the Fossdyke Canal in Saxilby was chosen, providing much needed employment in the village for over a century.

As this chapter begins, Saxilby Methodists were all worshipping in their newly built Centenary Chapel and had large congregations at all the services, but by 1852, due to various changes which had been occurring within movement, Saxilby had three chapels, all different branches of Methodism:

- The Wesleyans
- The Wesley Reformers *(became the United Methodist Free Chapel in 1857)*
- The Primitives

The Reform movement was particularly strong in this part of the country and according to the class membership records of 1851 around 60% of members in Saxilby had already left the Wesleyan chapel to join the Reform movement, which was a huge split. In some of the nearby villages congregations moved across from Wesleyan to the Reformers as a whole group, but in Saxilby the membership was divided.

As we know, the Primitive Methodist movement had started much earlier in the century, but it wasn't until 1852 that there was a society in Saxilby. Suddenly the village became a prime example of 'unity in diversity', with everyone being part of the Methodist Movement but diverging over the way they were governed and what could be done in individual chapels. We see members from different denominations working amicably together during the week but on Sundays worshipping in their own chapels and on weeknights meeting in their own class meetings, with numbers attending services growing at all three chapels.

The Keyworth family were part of the exodus to the Reform movement, becoming life-long members of what became known as the United Methodist Free Church. Martin and Sarah Keyworth from the Mill at Broadholme ensured their children all attended Sunday School at the Reform/Free Methodist chapel. They had five daughters and three sons.

Their eldest son Martin, born in 1847, became a Sunday School teacher, the chapel's librarian as well as singing in the choir, but tragically died of a fever at the age of 17. His obituary talks of his sweetness of disposition, his endearing nature, as well as his love of God right to the end of his life.

Their eldest daughter Rebecca, my great-grandmother, married William Drury, whose father had come to the village to farm when his wife had died in 1850. They lived at the farm house where 'Oaklands' now stands and William was a prominent figure in Saxilby Methodism throughout his life. Their five children all attended Sunday School at the Free chapel and became members of the society and will feature in future chapters.

Picture shows William Drury (my great-grandfather) in his horse and trap. He was a much respected local preacher, connected with both the Wesleyan Chapel and the Free Chapel and would go out taking services around the circuit with his violin, which he used to accompany the hymns if there was no harmonium.

Daughter Eliza was housekeeper to her step-brother George Howard until she married Richard Marshall. He became a farmer and cattle dealer on Mill Lane, and their children all attended Sunday school.

Meanwhile Martin's brother William who had taken over the family's butchery business on the High Street, went on to have 12 children, all going to Sunday School, with two of his sons, Robert and William Henry, becoming butchers.

Robert, born in 1859, married Harriet Ancliff, a farmer's daughter from Broadholme, at the Free Methodist chapel in Saxilby in 1886. He was known as Bob Keyworth and he and his wife lived in one side of Bedlam Cottages (now known as Bedlam Hall). They had one son William Edward, as well as an adopted son, John William Barker.

William Henry Keyworth, born in 1862, married Betsy Taylor from Doddington in 1881. At the time the Free Chapel in Saxilby did not have a licence for weddings, so they married at the Free Methodist Chapel in Silver Street, Lincoln, which was the main chapel of the circuit. He was affectionately known as 'Bill Henry Keyworth' and did much for the chapel, including always being in charge of auctioning the sale of the harvest produce at the Monday evening meeting. They had eight children who all attended Sunday School

As the congregations across the country grew larger, it became necessary to embark on huge building campaigns, with grand chapels being erected in all the large towns. In Lincoln a big 'Free Methodist' church was opened in 1864 on Silver Street, with pointed façade, the grand 'Portland Place' Primitive Methodist opened in 1874 on the High Street, and the 'Hannah Memorial' Wesleyan Chapel was erected at the corner of Chaplin Street and High Street in 1875. All were elegant, with pillars, some with galleries and capable of seating huge congregations and whilst Saxilby's three chapels of this period didn't match these imposing buildings in size, they certainly followed the trend in making them distinctive and attractive.

The Wesleyan Methodist Church
(which stood on the site of Richard Forman's car sales)

As we know, the Wesleyan chapel was built in the village in 1839 to commemorate John Wesley's conversion, a century earlier, called the Centenary Chapel to house the growing congregations flocking to Methodism in the early part of the century and was much larger in size than the original building of 1811. The *Stamford Mercury* dated 14 June 1839 reported that tenders for this new, much larger Wesleyan chapel were examined and the lowest tender amounting to £370 by Holland & Smith of Lincoln was accepted.

However, following the national picture, numbers in Saxilby reduced dramatically when the Reformers broke away but although demoralised, the Wesleyan chapel survived and their services continued with a regular Sunday School, choir, bible classes and a women's weekly meeting. Although the membership here remained quite low for about ten years, the congregations gradually increased as new initiatives within the Wesleyan movement became part of chapel life.

In 1856 the 'Home Mission' venture was launched, building on the concept of the 'Overseas Missionary Society', which had been established in 1813 to spread the Gospel abroad. The Home Mission venture concentrated on John Wesley's message of looking after those in need in this country. People in each chapel were assigned roles to promote both Home Missions and Overseas Missions during the year and it proved successful in raising the work of the church within the community as well as funds for this important work.

Inside the Wesleyan Chapel you see the raised pulpit with railings marking the communion table, the organ to one side and the choir benches just in front

There followed the endorsement within the Wesleyan movement of the temperance cause. John Wesley had always maintained that excessive drinking led to social problems and the destruction of family life, and this message fitted in with the objectives of the home mission society. 'Bands of Hope' were created which were connected to Sunday schools, where children could be taught the principle of abstinence. Soon all chapels in the village had a Temperance Society and a Band of Hope, with many members 'signing the pledge'.

Within twenty-five years of the Reform movement splitting away, the Wesley chapel was flourishing once again as the Chapel Anniversary celebrations of 1875 were reported in the Lincolnshire Chronicle. The preacher on that occasion was the Rev. H Codling from Grimsby, and it seems the chapel was full to almost overflowing as he was known to many of the congregation, having attended Sunday School when living in Saxilby as a boy.

Apparently the evening congregation was very large, larger than had been seen at the chapel at a service for many years. It was the same on the Monday when the usual public tea was held in the schoolroom, followed by a public meeting and concert in the chapel with Mr Strawson of Lincoln presiding over the event with music and singing as the main entertainment. The chapel was packed to the doors for the event, with every available space being used, including the communion area, the pulpit and the aisles. I think you could say it was full to the rafters! The choir was accompanied by Mr Smith of Harby on his violin and Mr Wright on the harmonium and their concluding piece was Handel's Hallelujah Chorus, which apparently the choir sang most heartily. In one of the pauses, the gravity of some in the audience was rather disturbed by a 'rustic' exclaiming in rather a loud tone, 'It's as hard work as threshing!'

In 1880-85 the chapel which stood towards the top of the High Street underwent restoration and renovations to rival the other denominations of Methodism in the village, with an extra room on the side added for the Sunday School and weekday meetings.

Wesley Reform Union/United Methodist Free Church
(*The 'Frees'*)
(now the Village Hall)

Whilst we have no exact details, the reform movement appears to have happened very quickly in the village sometime around 1849/50, mirroring what was happening throughout the country. It involved a sizeable number of the Wesleyan members leaving and forming a Reform society, initially using the old original chapel of 1811 in Chapel Yard, until a new place of worship could be built.

The site for this new chapel was at the junction of High Street and Sykes Lane, and it opened in February 1851. The Stamford Mercury reported that Mr Joshua Roberts preached at both services on the Sunday and a social party took place on the following day. About one hundred people sat down to the tea, which was followed by a public meeting with an address by Mr Roberts, followed by 'various acts of Methodist usurpation and misrule'.

Mr. William Conyers, who had done so much to aid the Methodist movement in the village during the earlier years, was someone who found great passion in the Reformer movement and when the new chapel in Saxilby was established, he presided over meetings in Gainsborough to set up a Wesley Reformer chapel there, 'finding a most favourable reception'. It appears the local press were not too pleased with any idea of reform, staunchly defending the established Wesleyan Methodists.

By 1857 many of the reform movements joined together to become the United Methodist Free Church, and from now on this chapel became known within the village as the 'Frees' and the size of the congregations at all services increased.

In July 1866 the Lincolnshire Chronicle reported that the UMFC had asked to purchase land of approximately 170 square yards belonging to the Parish, as they wanted to build an extension for the Sunday School. Parishioners agreed to sell it at 1s per yard.

As the number of people attending the Free Chapel kept increasing they needed extra space, and in 1881 a new and very grand place of worship was erected. It had an ornate sculptured façade with high windows to let in extra light, a large arched window facing the High Street and five arches either side of the main body of the church, with small round stained glass windows. The pews were in the central body of the church with aisles either side, the pulpit was raised up in front of the congregation to one side, with the choir sitting on the other side and the organ in pride of place in the centre,

The organ was specially commissioned for the new chapel, with local firm `Henry Jackson` who had a factory in Spa Buildings, Rosemary Lane, Lincoln, and is described in Laurence Elvin's book 'The Story of some North Country Organ Builders' as 'an instrument of delightful tone'.

The UMFC ready for a Harvest Festival, with the new organ in the centre

When the new chapel opened in 1881 it could seat 282 people and was described in the Lincolnshire Chronicle as a handsome place of worship in the 'Queen Anne style'. In keeping with the Arts & Crafts architecture of the time, it had fine windows and brickwork with stone or plaster trimmings and the very distinctive curved 'Dutch' gables.

The article also described the celebrations to mark the opening of this grand building, which were held on Wednesday 18th May 1881 when a large marquee was a erected in a nearby paddock, kindly provided by Mr G H Capes, enabling about 300 people to sit down to a public tea, reported as 'an excellent repast'. After tea there was a concert given by the choir, who were on excellent form, with Mr Smith of Harby conducting. The entire proceedings were very well received and the generosity of many friends, especial old scholars of the Sunday School, who now held positions within the big manufacturing companies, were acknowledged with thanks.

The services continued on the following Sunday when the Rev W L Lang preached in the morning and the veteran local preacher, Mr Thomas Nicholson of South Carlton, in the evening, with both services well attended with generous collections.

The usual public tea for over a hundred people followed on the Monday when all food was given, meaning the entire proceeds could be devoted to the building funds. Afterwards there was a meeting presided over by Mr William Conyers of Harby, with Rev. Lang, Alderman Easton Cottingham and Mr William Keyworth all giving excellent addresses.

The following weekend Rev R D Maud and Rev C H Butcher took the services on the Sunday to bring the celebrations to a close. The grand sum of £53 had been collected over the opening, taking the total sum raised so far to £292. There was still a long way to go to achieve the cost of the whole premises, which was £850 (over £110,000 today).

Primitive Methodist Church (Prims)
(on the site where the Fire Station now stands)

Although the Primitive Methodist movement had started nationally in 1807, there had been no society in Saxilby until 1852, when the first Primitive congregation began, initially using the building of the original chapel in Chapel Yard, recently vacated by the Reformers.

In 1875 they erected their own small chapel on a site at the bottom of the High Street and then virtually doubled the size of the chapel in 1888 with an extension which came right up to the roadside, featuring a pointed façade and a tall rounded window.

As explained earlier, the 'Prims' (as they became known) were very different in their method of worship and were more vocal in the political implications of their Christian faith, making them a quite separate organisation from the other denominations. It was within the Primitive movement that Trade Unions began, and from there the Labour Party gained much support.

Everyone was considered an equal in the Prims and they would address each other as 'brother' or 'sister'. Their services were always spontaneous, with no formal pattern of worship, and their preachers were renowned for their 'hellfire' sermons, leaving their congregation in no doubt that unless they changed their ways, the fiery wrath of God awaited them. No wonder they had the nick-name 'ranters'.

In Saxilby the Primitive Methodist Church was the last denomination to open a chapel and it's remembered as having smaller congregations, but they did have some very keen and enthusiastic members who ensured the chapel survived and flourished.

Their type of Methodism meant they were more culturally distinct than the Wesleyans and the Frees, who, despite disagreeing on the way they were governed, retained a close alignment on their style of worship, leading to a cooperation between the two chapels, whereas the Prims continued to keep themselves apart.

It should be mentioned that just as all the chapels were constructing or extending their buildings, the Church of England decided to build a church in the centre of the village on the High Street in 1879. It was known as St Andrew's Mission Church and was often used on a Sunday evening so that the members of the established church did not have the arduous task of climbing to the top of the village to worship in St. Botolph's. The church could seat 300 parishioners. It had eight large oil lamps hanging from the roof, with a chandelier providing light for the altar and it had its own organ, which was operated by a hand pump.

The chapter closes around 1880, with Saxilby having a population of just over 1000 but there were five places of worship, all being well attended and in active use but also in regular use, were four public houses and a beer house!

Chapter 4

1880-1900: Respectability and New Opportunities

The community continued to enjoy the changes and enrichment new people were bringing to the village, with fishermen arriving by train in huge numbers to fish on the Fossdyke. They required both refreshments and sometimes overnight accommodation, which the four public houses provided. The Sun and The Ship stood on the side of the canal, but in order to compete for trade, the Masons Arms changed its name to the Station Hotel and the Railway Hotel changed its name to The Anglers. There were some areas of disagreement between the teetotal Methodists and the pubs, with all three denominations involved in appealing to the local Magistrates not to allow extra licensing hours, but by and large the community existed quite harmoniously.

Fishermen arriving from Sheffield by train flock down the High Street on a Sunday morning towards the canal

Boat trips on the steamboat *Baltic* were a regular occurrence, travelling to the Pyewipe every Sunday morning, afternoon and evening and would even take 'pleasure parties'. Meanwhile Great Northern Railways was offering cheap excursions to London, departing Saxilby at 9.56am, as well as excursions to Leeds, Wakefield and Bradford, where passengers could visit a pantomime. There was also free passage offered for 'bone fide' farm labourers and domestic servants to emigrate to Queensland, Australia, boarding at Saxilby for onward travel on the next ship.

All three chapels in the village were extremely well attended, with various events taking place throughout the week, as well as Sunday services, and although most gatherings were primarily religious in content, concerts and other social events were greatly enjoyed by the large congregations and of course music played a huge part. Methodists have always had a reputation for their rousing singing and people would often say you could tell a Methodist by his singing. Hymns were likened to practical theology, whereby people would be singing them at home and at work, with the words constantly reminding them of the love of God and were really successful way of spreading Methodism across the country. Certainly in Saxilby you could guarantee they were always sung at speed and with enthusiasm.

However if you wanted to get married within the Methodist movement during this period, especially living in a small village like Saxilby, things weren't straightforward. Until 1837 all marriages had to take place in the Church of England. However, after that date some Methodist chapels were allowed to become registered for marriage, but the district registrar had to attend. In Saxilby records show that people attending the chapels would usually get married in Lincoln at the large chapel where the minister-in-charge of their chapel would be based, although a registrar would have been there to record the marriage. The Marriage Act of 1898 allowed non-conformist ministers to register marriages and in my own family this allowed my great-grandfather William Drury to officiate at his youngest daughter's marriage as a designated official,.

All chapels were self-funding. In contrast to the financial

security parish churches enjoyed with wealth accrued from church lands and properties, chapels had taken on huge debts with their ambitious building programmes. So there were always many special events laid on for fund-raising purposes, organised by all the denominations, which were greatly enjoyed. As you read about some of these events in the three Saxilby chapels, reported in the local papers at the time, you'll see they follow a similar theme with public teas at virtually every event, evening meetings with inspirational speakers and musical concerts. The fund raising is something that runs continuously through the book, as Methodists were always raising money, either for their own funds or for other charities, it was a way of doing good whilst socialising.

Wesleyan Methodist Church
(known as the Wesleyans)

The Wesleyans were always regarded as being closest to the Church of England in their thinking; only ordained Ministers could conduct marriages, funerals and baptisms and offer sacrament. In Saxilby they were often described as the 'high chapel' with their services being more structured and the local preachers more educated, as well as being the original home of Methodism in the village.

Funds had always been raised in the Wesley Chapel by renting out seats to those who could afford to pay. In the accounts book covering the years 1885-1896 there were 17 rows rented on both sides of the chapel and you paid 1/- per seat each month or 1/6 depending on where the row was situated. Names such as William Hardy, George Godfrey, John Skipworth, Edward Pantry, James Brumby Middleton and John Forrington are regular names throughout the period and the price never changed. Obviously for people like the Forrington family who had a number of children, they were paying 18/- per month, which was an enormous contribution to the trust funds.

The Wesleyan Chapel, with Sunday School on the side and front porch.

The Lincoln North Schedule book gives details of the Trustees of the chapel following restoration in 1885 showing just how many different people were involved and not just from Saxilby, Trustees were appointed to oversee the chapels and to safeguard their use for Methodist purposes and they were often quite powerful and wealthy men. Many Methodist business owners from Lincoln were happy to support their colleagues in Saxilby, including Joseph Collingham (Draper/later to form Mawer & Collingham), George Holmes (Grocer), John Battle (Chemist) and William Barnaby (Grocer). Local people included William Drury (farmer), John Wilson (shoemaker) and Edward Harris (farmer).

Special celebrations took place at the grand opening in October 1885, as reported in the local newspapers, when the commodious chapel was re-opened, having been repaired, decorated and a handsome porch built over the front entrance.

About 130 friends from Lincoln attended the event on a specially chartered train, thanks to the kindness of local JP Mr John Smith, who was a prominent Lincoln grocer and a Wesleyan local preacher. He obviously wanted to ensure the celebrations were well attended!

Mr Joseph Collingham JP (one of the Trustees of the chapel) opened a sale of work in the schoolroom, after which there was an afternoon meeting, presided over by Mr W W Richardson, the ex-sheriff of Lincoln. He informed the gathering that the refurbishment had cost almost £250 (about £37,000 today) and as the cash-in-hand was only just over £80, he hoped everyone would give generously.

As always a public tea took place, but to accommodate the large numbers it had to be held in a nearby barn, kindly lent for the occasion by a member of the chapel.

In the evening a large congregation gathered to hear

the Rev Charles Garrett who was an eminent temperance speaker, and one of the most popular Wesleyan ministers.

Because the Wesleyans were supported by such a network of wealthy and powerful individuals, as well as having such a sizeable income from the seat rents, it appears they felt somewhat superior. A suggestion of this superiority is expressed later in the book when the circuit issue is trying to find a resolution.

It was customary to hold anniversaries each year for the various groups within each society and perhaps one of the most important of these events was the Chapel Anniversary. In March each year the Wesleyan Chapel would hold special services to commemorate the start of the Society and in 1897 the anniversary took place when Mr. G Holmes of Lincoln came to preach at both services as reported in the Lincolnshire Chronicle. The usual public tea took place in the schoolroom on the Monday evening, followed by a lecture given in the chapel, entitled 'The good old times that our forefathers lived in, a century or more ago'. Mr William Drury, the local senior steward, gave the report and Mr Joseph Collingham JP of Lincoln presided over the meeting. It seems the idea of looking back at times gone by with rose-coloured spectacles doesn't change!

United Methodist Free Church
(usually referred to as the 'Frees')

The Free Chapel in the village was one that had split

from the Wesleyans and continued to attract a mixture of people from all parts of the community, including farmers and tradespeople, who ensured the society gained respectability.

When the new building had been completed in 1881 the Society Steward was Mr George Gilbert, a grocer's assistant living on the High Street. There were three local preachers on the UMFC plan from Saxilby at the time:

1. Mr William Rawding, a farmer at Ingleby, although his brother Henry Rawding (also a farmer) still worshipped at the Wesley Chapel.

2. Mr John Wilson, a shoemaker in the village.

3. Mr William Drury, farmer from the village, who also preached at the Wesleyan Chapel

In the Lincoln UMFC Circuit at the time there were just two appointed Ministers. The Rev W L Lang, who was the Superintendent Minister, was based at the Silver Street Chapel and the Rev R D Maud at Portland Street Chapel. As well as the two main chapels they had 21 village societies under their care, meaning every local chapel had to rely on lay preachers to take most of their services.

The Frees were very fortunate to have the Rev William Lockwood Lang as the designated minister for Saxilby. He'd been brought up in Cornwall, where his father was a farmer, and had been a Methodist minister for many years serving throughout Cornwall, with its small rural communities, so he was well used to villages like Saxilby. He moved to the area around 1880, just as the new 'Free' Methodist chapel was built, and was remembered as a wonderful preacher with a keen sense of fun. His wife was an active member in her own right, becoming a respected councillor, and they had seven children.

Rev Wm Lang with sons Dickerson & Norman 1884

Rev William Lang and sons Dickerson and Norman, 1884

The type of special meetings held at the Free chapel were wide and varied, designed to stimulate and educate, in fact as the Lincolnshire Echo reported, there were some quite in-depth topics, as the lecture below explains!

In 1893 Mr G B Setchfield of Lincoln came to give a mid-week lecture on the subject of 'Brain Structure and Functions'. The lecturer showed how the human mind adapted to Christianity, as well as explaining how the atonement of Christ coincided with man's nature. He finished off with advice on training the faculties in both children and adults. It appears there was a large audience, who showed their appreciation by the sizeable collection which was collected for chapel funds.

The schoolroom was also used for public meetings and in 1884 a group of 'liberal minded' people gathered under the chairmanship of Mr Henry Rawding, a tenant farmer, who spoke about reforming the land laws and protection against exorbitant rents. The organising secretary for Lincolnshire, Mr Harris, spoke about getting the franchise and went on to congratulate the agricultural labourers and artisans on their admission to their rights as English citizens. The large audience cheered with enthusiasm and went on to elect Mr Rawding as the chairman of the new Liberal Association, with Mr William Hardy (carpenter) as secretary and Mr Edmund Ancliff (farmer from Broadholme) as treasurer. Elections were then held for an executive committee made up of 12 members, with an equal number of farmers, tradesmen and agricultural labourers, ensuring every voice would be heard.

The arrival of the Lang family ensured that the Free Methodist chapel in Saxilby continued to thrive as their son, Dickerson Lang and his wife moved into Rose Villa on Lincoln Road to bring up their family. Dick (as he was known) was a director of the Henry Le Tall mill on the side of the Brayford and the whole family did an enormous amount of work for both the Methodist Movement and the wider community. He became a JP as well as serving on the local Parish Council, whilst his mother was the area's Rural District Councillor for many years.

The Free Methodist Church, built in 1881. The infant school can be seen at the side.

Easter was usually celebrated with a public tea on the afternoon of Good Friday, followed by a sacred concert, made up of music, recitations and dialogues appropriate to the occasion, which was always well supported. The mood changed for Sunday services when there would be special preachers and the joyful hymns celebrating the Easter story would be sung. Often there would be a special service of song in the afternoon.

The Primitive Church
(known as the Prims)

According to the Primitive Methodist quarterly guide 1895, Saxilby Prims had services every Sunday at 10.30am and

6pm, Sunday School at 2pm and a Wednesday meeting at 7pm once a month. Rev J Pearson of Newport Lincoln (the Minister-in-charge of the Lincoln Second Primitive Methodist Circuit) would be taking the services one Sunday each quarter and offering Sacrament at an evening service. There were 29 registered members, but the guide tells us there were healthy congregations at services. Assisting the Minister-in-Charge of Saxilby, were three lay preachers:

1. Mr William Nicholson, an agricultural labourer, who'd been born in Saxilby and now lived on the High Street with his wife Mary. He was the Society Steward, the senior person leading the chapel.

2. Mr Thomas Whittaker, who had moved to the area from Lancashire, was now living in the High Street with his niece/housekeeper, Agnes Briggs. He was a retired coal merchant and assisted the Society Steward.

3. Mr John Manning was a railway worker, living in Church Lane with wife Ann and daughter Agnes working as a dressmaker.

'Camp meetings' were a regular feature of Primitive Methodist life, always being held outdoors. They were an effective means of bringing the Gospel to as many people as possible. In Saxilby the camp meetings were usually just one-day events, commencing with a prayer in the chapel before moving outdoors. Once assembled the varied speakers would start addressing the crowds as loudly as possible, and there would be spontaneous prayers and rousing music and singing, trying to draw in the onlookers. Hymns were learned by rote and many in the crowds might never attend a service, but they would usually remember the hymns sung so joyfully. At the end of the day there would be a 'love feast' which involved the sharing of food and drink to remember the love of God at the last supper.

Saxilby Primitive chapel taken around 1890, you can see the original small building at the back, with the huge extension which was built in 1875. The photo shows the Sunday School celebrations, when they toured the village in drays with horses, singing anniversary songs.

Outdoor impromptu services were a regular feature of the Prims in Saxilby right into the 1940s when, after their evening services, the congregation would gather on the side of the canal and take the Christian message to the people who were drinking in both the Sun and the Ship, who often came out and dropped coins in the collection plate, strategically placed of course.

All the chapels had special services to celebrate Easter, usually starting with a sacred gathering on Good Friday. The local papers of 1897 recorded the Prims holding a public tea in the school-room with only a 'fair number sitting down'. They were then greatly entertained in the evening when Mr Joseph Warrener presided over a meeting in the chapel, which included various speakers and music by the choir. However I'm not sure the rendering of a humorous dialogue entitled 'Cookery and Good Advice' was appropriate for such an occasion, but gave amusement to everyone present.

Joseph Warrener was a farmer from Hardwick with a large family who all attended the Sunday school. He was a renowned speaker, who had a clever wit, was extremely humorous and was a committed member of the Primitive Chapel over many years, taking an active role in ensuring the worship at the chapel was successful.

The Primitives continued to chart their own way during this period, but the Frees and the Wesleyan Methodists were working quite closely together with both denominations having active Sunday Schools where the children were encouraged not only to learn of the love of God, but also to study and become self-confident through Sunday School activities. Previous Headteacher, Jack Daniels, gave the following quote in an article on the history of education in Saxilby:

In 1885 probably far more than half the people of Saxilby

were non-conformists with 53 children attended the Church of England Sunday School, whilst 170 children attended the two non-conformist Sunday Schools in the village.

Methodist Sunday Schools were always enjoyable, singing hymns written especially for children and stories of the bible being taught in a way that was easy for them to understand but there were also various anniversaries and outings to be enjoyed. Anniversary days were memorable in all the chapels with the children often having new clothes and performing poems and songs to large congregations of family and friends who applauded their efforts.

And then there was the annual gathering of the Non-Conformist Sunday School Union, eagerly anticipated by all the children each year. At the Whitsun weekend a fete would take place in Lincoln, with scholars from both the Wesleyan and the Free Sunday Schools in Saxilby taking part. On the Sunday, special services were conducted in all the local chapels connected with the event and in the year 1894 it was Mr. J T Forrington, farmer and grain merchant from the village, who chaired the special event which was held in the Saxilby Free Methodist chapel on the Sunday. The Lincolnshire chronicle gives us an account of the exciting happenings on the Bank Holiday Monday when the customary 'monstrous' procession took place.

Approximately 6500 children and teachers assembled at the Great Northern Station yard and spilled on to St Mary's Street before moving off along the High Street, Silver Street and Monks Road towards the Arboretum, led by the

Volunteer Band. There would have been thousands of gaily coloured banners and flags all ensuring the huge crowds who lined the streets enjoyed the procession. When they reached the Arboretum there were various games laid on for the scholars, the maze was open and apparently there was a conjurer for the little ones. The adults could listen to a drum and fife band contest before everyone enjoyed a wonderful tea which was held in a large marquee. In the evening balloons representing pigs, elephants and other animals were released, rising across the city's skyline, much to the delight of the youngsters.

Can you picture the excitement of children from a small village like Saxilby taking part in such a huge event, which would have started with a train outing into Lincoln before joining all the other children to march through the streets of Lincoln? Certainly it was always much enjoyed. The custom of joining the Sunday School celebrations continued for many years until the Prims started their own procession around the village, singing the anniversary songs to the community. The other two chapels then decided to follow suit and have their own celebrations, including riding round the village on horses and drays (wagons) on the Monday, followed by a tea with games on the Tuesday.

Young people have always played an important part in the life of any Methodist chapel and as the movement progressed, it led to the founding of The National Children's Home followed in 1896 by another association, originally started as a youth movement, called the Wesley Guild, aimed at countering secular influence and retaining young people within the church. The next chapter explores how both the Sunday Schools and the Guild played a big part in the life of all the Saxilby chapels during the early part of the 20th century.

By this point in time, the Methodist movement had become much more respectable, accepted both nationally and in the wider world as a dedicated and extremely well disciplined organisation, with strict guidelines for members to follow. Robert Wearmouth states in his book 'Methodism and the Common People' that it was this discipline that gave Methodists an air of 'respectability'. Because everyone was encouraged to speak freely and share their growing spiritual knowledge with each other, a bond of mutual understanding between members was created, ensuring that the sense of duty expected as part of being a Methodist, was used both within the life of the chapel – as stewards, class-leaders, Sunday School teachers or lay preachers – and also into the wider community with trades people gaining the reputation as reliable, dependable and of course sober. Indeed Methodism during this period chimed whole-heartedly with the ideals and values which had flourished during the reign of Queen Victoria - morality, duty, a strong work ethic and personal improvement.

Chapter 5

1901-1914: The Next Generations

The beginning of the 20th century is marked by the death of Queen Victoria in January 1901. The Queen had become almost a recluse during her latter years and when her son became King Edward VII, heralding the Edwardian Era, the country seemed to burst into new life, often referred to as the 'golden age'.

Architecture became less ornate and more functional, first with gas lighting, followed later by electricity and plumbing. Quite early into the new era we see notices advertising building plots for sale in Saxilby and during the next ten years there were many new properties built. Most of the houses were named 'villas' and most were built for renting out. In 1910 the cost of renting a semi-detached villa with excellent garden and orchard in a central village position would cost £14, but if you wanted a bathroom with hot and cold water in a semi-detached villa near the church, the cost would be £20 per annum! Detached houses would be around £25 to rent. When walking round the village today, you can see the examples of this period of architecture, usually built in pairs, all called names such as 'Riverlin Villas' or 'Glen Villas'.

The villas built down West Bank, Saxilby, in the early 1900s

In fact, considerable building development took place when new manufacturing companies came to Saxilby. The motor car was becoming a more common sight around the village and in 1904 J. R. Richardson Co. (Lincoln) Ltd opened a new motor works at Saxilby covering an area of 10,000 sq. ft. with electric lighting throughout provided by its own private plant and employing a good number of local people, who received training in the manufacturing of cars. An advertisement in the Lincolnshire Chronicle of 1904 read:

'In case of breakdown, send a telegram to 'Motor, Saxilby' and a relief car with competent and experienced man with full kit of tools will effect a roadside repair or a tow if the problem is unable to be fixed.'

Unfortunately for the motor works, the company over-stretched itself and went into liquidation only two years after opening, but the good news for Saxilby was that their site was quickly snapped up by a manufacturing company looking to relocate from Southward Bridge in London because of the high overheads in the capital. The Lincolnshire Chronicle of December 1906 carries a lengthy write-up on why the well-established company of H. J. West & Co. Ltd moved to Lincoln. They were mainly refrigeration engineers making machinery for brewers, dairymen and butchers and were more than willing to take on most of the workforce from the car manufacturing company, as they were already skilled in manufacturing. By 1907 over 200 people were being employed as the site became fully operational.

Members of all the three Methodist chapels in Saxilby benefitted from the influx of people coming to work on the railways or in other new businesses. As the Edwardian Era arrives, many of the sons and daughters, who had all attended Sunday school, married locally, now become active both in the chapels and within the community.

John Skipworth was such an example. He moved to Saxilby with his wife Jane and young family in 1883 initially as a railway platelayer before becoming gatekeeper for many years. He quickly joined the chapel and soon became a prominent figure in the Wesleyan Chapel. In the minute book of Local Preachers from 1897, he became an 'exhorter', which was the first stage of becoming a local preacher. A new exhorter would usually work with an experienced preacher, rather like an apprentice.

His wife Jane was well known in the village in her role of 'emergency nurse', giving care to all who needed help without payment. There was an occasion reported in the Retford & Worksop Herald in 1914 when a pram rolled into the water down West Bank with a baby inside. The mother waded into the river and managed to pull the baby out, but the child appeared dead. Mrs Skipworth was sent for and thanks to her resuscitation, the little one rallied. Jane was highly respected throughout the community, as many such acts of help and care were common place, with all the villagers contributing to a collection for her when she retired.

John's stepson, Charles Wright Oxby, was 12 years old when they moved, but as soon as he was old enough, he too got work on the railway as a platelayer. Having been a regular at the Sunday School, he soon became a member of the chapel, attending services and becoming secretary for the newly formed Wesley Guild in 1904-05. It was there he met his future wife, Nellie Drury (daughter of William Drury) and they married in 1905 and set up home down West Bank, where they lived all their lives. Their two children, William and Jessie, attended Sunday School at the Free Chapel and became members of the society.

His daughter Edith taught in the Sunday school as well as taking part in various musical entertainments. In fact, she was still attending the chapel and teaching in Sunday School when I was a child in the 1950s. The older members of the Sunday School would call at her cottage on the High Street and push her to the chapel in her wheelchair.

As we explore the life of the chapels in the early part of the 20th century, there are many names that may well seem familiar even today, because, like the Skipworth-Oxby-Drury example, people would marry locally, often within the Methodist family, and the generations carried on, ensuring all three chapels in Saxilby continued to thrive.

The Valley family had been staunch members at the Wesley Chapel since coming to the village late in the 1870s. John Valley had found work as a gardener's labourer and moved to Saxilby with his wife Mary, raising a large family of five boys and five girls. By the 1900s, John had become a market gardener living down Lincoln Road, and all their children attended the Wesleyan Chapel, with some settling down in the village to make their living.

Their son, Joseph Turner Valley, left school at the age of 12 and worked on his father's fields for many years, earning the sum of half-a-crown at the age of 30, before marrying Louisa Wilson, who was very musical and played the organ at the chapel for many years. Joseph himself became a renowned local-preacher as well as President of the Lincoln

Society of Methodists

William Julian had moved to the village in 1890 as a railway porter after being widowed. He then married local girl Louise Atkinson, whose father was a shepherd at Ingleby, and they brought up two daughters, Constance and Gwendolen, from William's first marriage, as well their own two sons, William and George, all attending Sunday School at the Wesleyan.

William Long moved to the village as a postman in the early 1900s and lived in William Street; he was very musical, playing the trumpet and the organ at services. They had a son, Jack, and three daughters, Dora, Winifred and Alma, who all attended Sunday School, going on to become teachers. Alma later married Jack Hauton from the Free Chapel.

My grandmother, Minnie Keyworth Drury, was the daughter of William Drury who had been the senior steward at the Wesleyan Chapel for five decades, but followed her mother's family and attended the Free Chapel, which is where she met Joseph Vasey, who had come to Saxilby as an apprentice plumber with Mr Smith of Bridge Street. They got married in 1903 and had two daughters, Connie and Gladys, living on Lincoln Road, with Joe setting up his own plumbing business from the yard. Joe would travel miles in his horse and cart to sink wells for people in their fields and gardens, and was adept at water divining, using a hazel twig he always carried; I remember watching him with fascination when I was very young. He was also skilled at lead work and spent many hours at Doddington Hall working on the lead roof which covers the spires.

Grandma Vasey kept chickens in the long garden behind their house and sold the spare eggs to a co-operative who would call round each week to collect them. Their life revolved around work and the chapel, with Grandpa Vasey getting much of his work from members within the Methodist movement and Grandma frequently entertaining visiting preachers.

Grandma's brother Charlie Drury had his own farm in Broadholme from an early age, with his sister Nellie keeping house for him until he married local farmer's daughter Jane Ancliff. They had three sons, although their middle boy, Laurence, was killed in 1918 in Flanders.

Grandma's sister, Annie, married local cattle dealer George Sargeant and lived in a house (with an attached yard) on the High Street, opposite the butcher's shop belonging to Bill Henry Keyworth. They moved to a farm near Stow, where their one daughter Lillian grew up and were regular members at the chapel there. Lillian married Albert Wattam and ran the Post Office in Stow for many years.

By 1915 the next generations of the Drury grandchildren were all attending Sunday School and became life-long members of the Methodist Church.

Members of all the chapels also involved themselves in village life, with Mrs Caroline Lang (wife of the Rev Wm Lang) being elected as one of the Rural District Councillors representing the village for many years. On the Parish Council of 1901, six out of ten elected councillors were Methodists:-

1. The Chairman was Mr John Turner Forrington, who was a local farmer and corn merchant. He married Annie Lee, a Miller's daughter from Newark and they had a large family who were much involved in the life of the *Wesleyan Chapel*, contributing generously to the work of the church.

John Turner Forrington and his wife Annie

2. Mr Dickerson Lang JP, a prominent figure at the Free Chapel, who took the lead on many projects in the village, such as 'considering ways and means of providing a village hall for Saxilby', as well as corresponding with the County Council on the matter of enforcing the speed limit in the village to curb the fast and furious motoring by some!

3. Mr William Drury, local farmer married to Rebecca Keyworth, and senior steward at the Wesleyan Chapel for many years, as well as being a local preacher.

4. Mr James Hauton, market gardener from Mays Lane, long-time member of the Free Chapel.

5. Mr Thomas Whittaker, coal dealer, who was the driving force at the Primitive Chapel and Society Steward there for many years.

6. Mr Robert Keyworth, butcher, married local farmer's daughter Harriet Ancliff, a member of the Free Chapel. Grandson of John & Rebecca Keyworth, who were members of the first Saxilby Chapel back in 1808.

The Clerk to the Council was Mr Edward Pantry, who served for many years, earning just over £20 per annum. He had moved to the village in 1870s as a tailor, joining the Wesley Chapel where he took charge of the choir, marrying Elizabeth Colley/Harrison, a school teacher in the village, who had been brought up by her grandparents William and Mary Harrison, who had been a blacksmith in Saxilby.

The halcyon days of massive congregations seen

during the 1870s-1890s gradually began to give way to membership numbers which, whilst very sizeable, enabled closer connections between members within each chapel, rather like one huge family, with everyone knowing all about each other. Services became a time of coming together to sing and worship together with friends. Co-operation between the Free Chapel and the Wesleyan Chapel became even closer, with joint musical events and ventures involving members from both chapels coming together. In 1906 a joint choir from Saxilby Frees & Wesley Chapels entered the Kettlethorpe choir competition and won!

Photo of the combined choir in 1906 includes: Louise Julians, Charles Oxby, Joe Vasey, Ada Little, Rose Poole, Minnie Vasey.

Christmas Day in the 'chapel family' was a special occasion which went back over many decades with different denominations always holding something of an event, sometimes at their own chapels and occasionally joining together. The Retford & Worksop Herald gave a report on the Christmas Day celebrations of 1906 when the Primitive Methodists held their annual Christmas Day event. The festivities commenced in the afternoon with the Christmas Tree being decorated, gifts from the bran tub and various stalls including hoopla for the children. After the usual public tea, a service was held in the chapel with friends from the other chapels helping provide a varied programme. It seemed an incredibly long affair as the choir sang eight carols, there were three duets, one recitation and eight solos, all given by familiar names from the different chapels, with Mr Pantry (Wesleyan) conducting and Miss Smalley (Wesleyan) and Mrs Vasey (Frees) accompanying. Mr Warrener (Prims) was presiding. However, we must remember there was no television or other forms of entertainment and obviously everyone enjoyed being part of the Methodist family on Christmas Day.

A new and successful organisation was started at the Wesleyan Chapel in 1905 called the Wesley Guild, which had been launched by the Wesleyan Association at the end of the last century, aimed at keeping young people within the church once they were too old for Sunday school. The Guild motto was *One Heart ~ One Way* and took the form of a weekly meeting on a Wednesday evening running throughout the winter months. Membership was defined as follows:

- Active Members are people who are members of the church and wishful to help others.

- Companion members are young people who wish to join any section of the Guild and who are in sympathy with its spirit of friendship and service.

- Associate members are older members and friends who are in sympathy with the movement.

Initially the programme followed a regular four-weekly pattern in the form of 'Christian Service", 'Literary', 'Social' and finally at the end of each month 'Devotional', with a monthly Devotional meeting running right through the summer. Officers were appointed annually with a leader, a secretary and a committee to organise each section of the programme and we see from the names on the printed card of 1907-08 that the next generation of members were very active. William Drury's two daughters, Nellie and Rebecca, now Mrs Oxby and Mrs Vasey, Ed Pantry's son Percy and his wife-to-be Zilpah Topliss and many of the younger Valley family were on various committees.

The first 'social' event in February 1905 attracted a good attendance with a programme of songs, readings and a recitation, together with musical selections on the gramophone by Mr G. H. Marshall. Refreshments were provided by the social committee and everyone felt it was a thoroughly enjoyable event. On a later occasion, Mr Atkinson from Lincoln brought friends over to entertain the large company. The season closed on the 19th May with a Devotional meeting, when an address was given by Mr Julians entitled 'Knowing Christ'. The Guild weekly meetings were well attended by people from all three chapels as well as younger village folk, who liked what they heard about the meetings and came along and thoroughly enjoyed the varied programmes which included debates, drama productions, outings, carol singing and even holidays. The friendships built up at this society helped enormously when the different denominations of Methodism finally united in the 1930s.

About 30 years ago, when my daughter was doing a history project, I accompanied her as she interviewed several older members of the chapel, asking for their recollections, stories passed down from their parents, as well as attending chapel as young people. This means much of the history of the chapels around this period is anecdotal but research at Lincoln Archives and the local newspapers reports of the time, together with written contributions/memorabilia collected by the Saxilby History Society give a real flavour of the activities at the chapels and the people involved.

It would seem that around this time, the chapels became known as the Top Chapel (Wesleyan), the Middle Chapel (Frees) and the Bottom Chapel (Prims), presumably because of their locations on the High Street, although there was the inference from the ladies interviewed, that there may well have been a divide along the following lines:-

Top Chapel was the 'established/superior' chapel, where many of the dynastic families were members, rich farmers and of course Mr Godfrey, who was known to turn anyone out who dared sit in his pew!! It was also towards the top of the High Street!

The Middle Chapel encompassed the more liberal minded/middle-of-the-road/middle income people, attracting many of the trades people like the Hauton family, the Dennis family and my own family the Vaseys. Farmers like the Cottinghams from Broxholme as well as many smaller farmers from Broadholme, like the Ancliffs, and of course the Lang family from Rose Villa. It stood towards the centre of the village.

The Bottom Chapel was where the 'evangelicals/ workers' worshipped; they were very vocal in style and attracted people who enjoyed a more 'down to earth' service. This chapel was right at the end of the High Street, close to the Fossdyke Canal.

Some of the people we talked to even likened the chapels to the political movements, Conservatives, Liberals and Labour!

Certainly you were recognised in the village community by the chapel you attended, although the Guild meeting did much to aid closer relationships between all the chapels and the church over the years. The Sunday services at all three chapels appeared to follow a similar format, beginning with morning Sunday School at 9.30am, which then joined the 10.30am service. Afternoon Sunday School was at 2pm and then the evening service started at 6pm, often followed by a prayer meeting.

It was not uncommon at this time for older daughters to become housekeepers for their brothers or other family members before becoming married themselves, and my grandmother told me stories of how her sister went to keep house for her brother when he was farming at Broadholme, which involved a long walk along field paths to get to the village. As was the case at the time, no unnecessary chores were ever done on a Sunday, so meals had to be prepared on the Saturday. Her sister then walked to chapel in time for the service at 10.30am (having first put the joint in the oven), before walking back to the farm to get lunch on the table for 12.30pm. Back to chapel for Sunday School class at 2pm, then home to get tea for 4.30pm, before returning with her brother for 6pm service, although usually the horse and trap would be used in the evening. No washing-up was done on a Sunday; it was left until Monday morning!

Walking along these field paths today, seeing small farms dotted around the outer edges of the village, it's difficult to imagine just what it would have been like to walk these grass paths, often muddy, in your 'Sunday best', trying to keep clean and dry, no easy job I suspect.

During the next decade chapels continued to enjoy good congregations and held their many special anniversary services. The Middle/Free Chapel always had a Missionary Anniversary and invited speakers who had been missionaries in various countries, including East Africa and

China. These services attracted large congregations and any public meeting held during the week would always start with a missionary tea, which ensured good attendance. As the years went by entertainment was often in the form of lantern slides, illustrating the work of the missionaries in these far-away countries, which proved very popular and informative.

Most chapels would do a 'spring clean' each March/April time, and in the photograph below there is a rather eclectic team from the Wesleyan Chapel, standing outside with their buckets and brooms. There appears to be a nurse as well as a young lady with a dog. I'm not sure whether the ladies would keep their hats on to do the cleaning?

Spring cleaning at the Wesley Chapel

Mr & Mrs Lang from Rose Villa were regular hosts for Free Chapel events in their large garden, on one occasion having over 150 friends from the Lincoln chapels out to spend the day and enjoy refreshments. Garden parties became a regular occurrence at their house, usually raising money for the chapel, but always thoroughly enjoyable occasions with various types of entertainment. Young people from the chapel were encouraged to be independent and organise events and in June 1910 about 250 young people organised a tea on the lawn at Rose Villa, through the kindness of Mr & Mrs Lang, followed by a short programme of recitations and music, finishing with games and music from Mr Storey's gramophone.

In June 1913 there was a massive fete held in their garden in order to try to clear the remaining debt from the building of the Free Chapel back in 1881. The local press gave accounts of the event, explaining what a perfect day it had been, as the weather was warm and sunny. Mr Lang's brother and his wife travelled from Liverpool specially for the occasion, having been invited to open the event. There were a large number of stalls selling various items made by the Sewing group, an Aunt Sally game, shooting range, quoits as well as skittles and bowling for a live pig. It appears there was also an art gallery, but no details were given. Music was played during the afternoon by a string band. The fete finished with an excellent display of gymnastics by the Lincoln Technical School boys team. It was certainly an outstanding event, with enough money being raised to clear the outstanding debt on the building.

The Primitive Chapel obtained a licence for the solemnisation of marriages in 1910 and in November that year a large company assembled to witness the marriage of Mr Thomas E Ford, second son of Mr & Mrs Harry Ford of Sykes Lane and Miss Laura Groves, granddaughter of Mr & Mrs Thomas Groves of May's Lane. Her two younger sisters were bridesmaids and Mr Frank Ford, brother of the groom, was best man. The newly-wedded pair had both been connected with the Chapel, the Sunday School and the Choir for many years.

Harvest Festivals were held in all the chapels at the end of September with wonderful displays of fruit and vegetables and large congregations. They were known as 'harvest thanksgiving' and some superb hymn-singing always made the services seem special, decorated to reflect the end of harvest time. All the chapels followed a similar format of decorating their buildings on the Saturday, special preachers on the Sunday followed by a public tea and meeting on the Monday. At the close of the meeting, the fruit and vegetables would be auctioned for sale and any money raised aided church funds. There would also be chapel anniversary celebrations to mark another year of worship, with special speakers at the services on the Sunday and usually followed by a public tea on the Monday, with a meeting or concert to follow.

Ladies would meet regularly on a weekday afternoon for their own gathering, with no men allowed to cross the threshold, except for the Minister, who would occasionally be invited to speak to them. In the Prims, this meeting was known as the Bright Hour, in the Frees and the Wesleyans it was called the Sisterhood. There would be offshoots, like the Sewing Group, who would meet to make various items and then hold a 'sale of work' again raising funds for the chapel. On occasions the ladies would hold a threepenny tea before meetings, where cakes would be available with cups of tea from huge silver teapots, always highly polished before such events.

Saxilby Band of Hope continued to meet regularly across all three chapels, and wherever the meetings were held, members went along to encourage and support the children, fostering yet more co-operation between the different establishments as members became better acquainted with each other. Events were always entertaining and children from all the different chapels would come together and be encouraged to perform recitations or sing, giving them confidence as well as enjoying being part of a large group.

All the people I talked to mentioned the Sunday School and what a part it had to play in the life of each chapel. In the late 1800s there were huge numbers of children in regular attendance at all three chapels and courtesy of the Saxilby History Society, there are beautiful hand-written registers from the Primitive Sunday School for 1902-03. Joseph Swingler, a local cycle-maker/repairer from Bridge Street, was the secretary at the time and organised about

75 children into different classes, following the age-related school groupings. There was a separate girls and boys class named 'infants' for 3-6 year olds and those aged 7-11 were in 'testament' classes, with those aged 12-16 in the 'bible' classes. Similar Sunday Schools took place at both the Middle Chapel and the Top Chapel, all teaching the children in age-related classes. Attendance was kept and at the end of each year, the children would be awarded prizes.

The highlight of the year of was course the Sunday School Anniversary, which was the climax of much rehearsing of songs and poems, when the children would perform to chapels packed to the rafters, as families would turn out in force to listen to the special service. By this time, instead of the Sunday School students travelling into Lincoln to join the big parade, the children stayed in Saxilby with each chapel having their own parade around the village. They had a special tea in their own schoolroom, usually consisting of bread and butter, potted meat, plum loaf and cups of tea, poured out from huge silver teapots, polished and gleaming, by the ladies of the chapel. Games like the egg & spoon race, three-legged race, rounders and cricket would follow in a farmer's field, followed by a parade around the village in horse-drawn carts and trailers, singing the songs from the anniversary, with members collecting coins from people as they watched. A harmonium would be hauled onto the leading cart to ensure the singing was in tune and enthusiastic.

This photo taken in 1927 shows some of the children from the United Chapel Sunday School in their dray waiting to set off to parade around the village. As you can see they were packed in tightly with little regard for safety!

Chapter 6

1914 to 1932: The War Years and Beyond

The war of 1914-18 was a rude awakening for the community, as young men who had enjoyed their times at Sunday School went off to fight for 'king and country' and in many cases didn't come home again. Various initiatives were set up in the village to assist the war effort, with working parties at the infant school for ladies of the village to come together and make up parcels for those serving overseas as well as for refugees, and all villagers being encouraged to contribute eggs to the National Egg Collection for wounded soldiers. In 1915 the Retford & Worksop Herald reported that although Saxilby had sent 89 soldiers to fight for the country in March they had only contributed 75 eggs!

Wounded soldiers arrived at Saxilby station from

Sheffield, where they were conveyed in motor vehicles to the Thorney Hall VAD Hospital. Mr Dick Lang was again active in the community, organising an event to collect money for the Widows & Orphans Fund. The Retford & Worksop Herald also reported on the visit of the Lincoln Branch of the N.U. Railwaymen Brass Band, who arrived by boat at Rose Villa before parading to the Parish Church for a service, with a collection taken en route. Mr Lang then presided over an open air service at the Crossing Foot at 6pm.

Services at all the chapels continued, with support given to members like Mr & Mrs Edmund Ancliff from Broadholme, whose son Frank went missing in the Dardanelles, and Mr & Mrs Charlie Drury, whose son Laurence was killed right at the end of 1918 on Flanders Field.

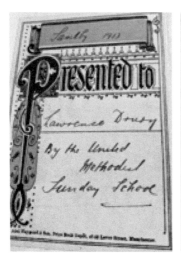

As these two pictures show, within five years of receiving his prize at the United Methodist Sunday School, young Laurence Drury, had joined the army but in 1918, Private L Drury 42453, 2nd Battalion Bedfordshire Regiment had died on Flanders Field, aged just 19.

William Butler and Tom Pocklington from the Primitive chapel and Robert Sims and Wilkinson Credland from the Wesleyan chapel never came home.

Herbert Valley survived the battle on the Somme and the dreadful ordeal of Passchendaele although if a shell which fell just three feet from his head had not failed to explode, he would not have returned home.

Fred Skipworth, son of John Skipworth, was injured by shrapnel early in 1916 and brought back to Northfield hospital in Birmingham, alongside many others who were injured in 'the great push'.

Whilst Mrs Ira Keyworth's grandson Harry loved the life as a driver in the RAF, Herbert Sutcliffe's nephew Walter hated being a solider in the Yorks & Lancs Regiment, especially the rain seeping into the tent, the physical drill and the very long marches.

It was a sad and worrying time, but the community came together and did what they could to help those who had suffered bereavement, as well as supporting those involved in the war.

The local papers reported various events which happened in the chapels to help the troops and to encourage and support their congregations during the time of conflict.

On New Year's Eve 1915/16 the young ladies of the United Methodist Church organised a social to raise money to provide 42 of the soldiers and sailors from the village with either a helmet or a pair of gloves. Replies received from some of the young men expressed pleasure and satisfaction with the gifts, saying how very nice it was to know that people at home were thinking about them.'

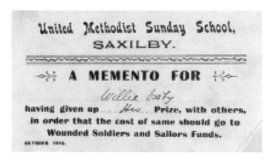

A large number of Sunday School children went without their prizes, the money going to help the wounded soldiers and sailors.

Fund-raising events such as concerts and rummage sales were held, all funds raised going towards helping the cause, but at the same time keeping members spirits up during such dark days.

The Band of Hope had a crowded attendance in the United Methodist Schoolroom when the winners of the recitation contest were announced, followed by one of the daughters of the Beivnaerts family (refugees from Belgium who were given shelter in the village) giving a recitation in Flemish. No one could understand a word, but it was appreciated by everyone.

Because Saxilby was a rural community many young men had to stay in the village to work the farms, grow the vegetables, bake the bread, supply groceries and other essentials, so chapel services continued to be well attended throughout this period. Harvest Festivals had huge congregations as the villagers came to give thanks for safe and bountiful harvests in such terrible times. Sunday School anniversaries continued with parents and friends coming to support their children as well as showing their appreciation of the work being done for their well-being during this period. The usual processions took place round the village with the scholars given tea, followed by games and sports in one of the local farmer's fields, helping lift the spirits for the village as stories of the terrible events of the war reached home.

As the conflict came to a close the village came together as a community and decided to raise a war memorial in memory of the men who had fallen during the Great War. A committee was formed incorporating various farmers and trades-people, of all denominations, to collect donations and in 1920 land was purchased for £800 in the centre of the village to open public grounds for the benefit of the inhabitants of Saxilby-cum-Ingleby and Hardwick for the rest-and-recreation of adults and as play grounds for the children. This was to be known as 'The Recreation Ground' under the management and control of a committee, to be known as 'The Management Committee'. This facility has been a lasting legacy and enjoyed over generations, indeed just as this book is being written, the building of a 'wheeled park' has been completed in one part of the field which will provide much enjoyment to the inhabitants of Saxilby for generations to come.

The village is fortunate that the Saxilby History Society has collected many records to chart the history of the village. As part of the collection, Rev. Norman Valley recounts the early years of his family coming to the village as well as his time as a young man in the 1920s-30s at the Wesleyan chapel and then his early days at the 'new' chapel. There is also written testimony from Harry Butler, who remembers his time at the Primitive Chapel. These stories combined with recollections and accounts from some of the older members, as well as my own family, give an insight of chapel life in the years after the war and how Methodism continued to appeal to people both in Saxilby and nationally.

The Wesleyan Church
(now often known as the Top Chapel)

From the written account by Rev Norman Valley, we know the Valley family always worshipped at the Wesleyan chapel since coming to the village in the late 1870s.

When John Valley died in 1923, his son Joseph took over the business and raised three sons, his eldest boy Norman, becoming a Methodist minister, his youngest son Donald training as a local-preacher, but it was the middle son, Bernard who carried on the Market Garden business down Lincoln Road, although he was connected with the Sunday School for many years, both as a teacher and treasurer.

Joseph's brother John Will Valley, was a regular chapel member, but much more of a 'fire-brand' than the rest of his family and several people of my generation remember him as a very small man but with a very loud voice, who would always say the Lord's prayer at least one line ahead of the preacher and sing at the top of his voice.

Herbert Valley, the youngest brother, served in the Royal Field Artillery during the war, marrying Dora Norman in 1924 and settling down in Mays Lane, raising son John and daughter Betty. All the family were regular chapel members. Herbert is remembered fondly as a softly spoken man who was a renowned beekeeper for over 60 years and wrote some wonderful poetry and I am very grateful to Betty (Hurst) Valley for keeping photographs and records of the family's involvement in the chapel, even though she herself was brought up attending the Church of England, only transferring her membership in 1956.

Norman mentions the wealthy families who attended the Wesley chapel including:

- The Hotchkin family from Hardwick, who always went to services at their own little chapel whenever they were held, but were very supportive of the Centenary Chapel. They employed people from the chapel whenever they could and continued to be great benefactors all their lives.

- Another farmer, Walter Hipkin from High Ingleby, who had a superb sense of humour and acted as a Trustee of the chapel for many years.

- Mr Jim Read, who had been a Captain in the first world war, lived at Martin Lodge on Church Road, was a regular member and very generous financially to the chapel, teaching several young people to play the organ. His sister married into the Sturdy family at Skellingthorpe, and their son Harry went on to become a Methodist minister

- The Miller family who had taken over Henry Read's shop when he moved the post office across the road to Walnut House. They had a large family, with their son Richard becoming a Methodist Minister and their daughters becoming Sunday School teachers and members of the Guild.

- Mr George Godfrey was another member who was generous with his money, living in Churchfield House (now the village veterinary centre) who had made his money being a 'coal and manure merchant' before becoming a farmer in later life. He never had any children, so left a sizeable part of his estate to enable the 'new' chapel to be built, provided it was named the Godfrey Memorial Methodist Church.

The United Methodist Free Church
(known as 'The Frees', now sometimes The Middle Chapel)

The choir here was already much renowned for introducing really high-class music to the area and continued to flourish under the direction of Mrs Charles, the butcher's wife, with people from the Wesleyans often coming to join in concerts or special events. The choir had numerous engagements and musical events, together with an annual outing sometimes using the train but in 1929 hired a bus to Matlock Bath in Derbyshire with some members managing the strenuous climb to the top of High Tor.

Choir outing to Matlock Bath 1929. Unfortunately many faces are unknown, but on the back row are Martin Drury, Gladys Vasey, and Charlie Oxby. on the front row in white dress is Gladys Poole, then seated is Jessie Oxby, Kathy Lang, Mary Little, Connie Vasey, Minnie Vasey, Jack Lang, with Joe Vasey at end of row. Marjorie Clark (Ford) is kneeling at the front.

Included in the choir were members of the Poole family who lived down Lincoln Road, with their father James, who was a small farmer. It was the younger children, Martin, Rose and Herbert, who came to the chapel in the 1920s, looking after their father when their mother died, with Martin continuing to live at home on Lincoln Road and never marry – affectionately known to many as 'Uncle Martin'. Rose married Joseph Ford, who worked at the Chemical Works, and continued to be a Sunday School teacher for many years, living in a cottage on Lincoln Road close to her brother.

Herbert worked as a horseman for the Cottingham family (members of the Middle Chapel) at their farm in Broxholme when he left school, but then found work with the drainage board when he married, having a daughter Gladys, who had many recollections of life as a young girl at the Middle Chapel. She sang in the choir and attended the Wesley Guild meetings, where she met her future husband John (Jack) Fox, whose family attended the Wesleyan Chapel, but they got married at the Free Chapel and their son Gerald was christened there.

The Middle Chapel was considered quite liberal-minded in these days, with Dick Lang and his wife ensuring speakers came to talk to packed meetings on a wide variety of topics.

According to The Retford & Worksop Herald, in 1927 a meeting was held in the Free Chapel to mark the visit of the Rev H Chatterton of Harrogate, where the speaker, Mr Arthur Neal (the prospective Liberal candidate for the Gainsborough Division) gave a thoughtful and very effective address on the subject of 'Practical Pity'. Whilst not necessarily putting forward his own political views, he explained that he considered religion and politics should not be divorced from each other. He went on to talk about how regular attendance at services on a Sunday might be counted as holy by some, it was the practical pity which was to be shown to the poor, who lived amongst us, that all Christians should care about. He ended his address by saying: 'if we cannot all be united either in church life, in social life or in political life, let us all be united in a great endeavour to do what is possible to make the world better than we found it'. The large audience showed their appreciative with much applause, and Mr Dick Lang thanked him for his thoughtful and considered lecture.

The congregations continued to be large and the chapel thrived financially, as they had many farmers and tradespeople as members. The Cottingham family, farmers from Broxholme, had been lifelong members of the chapel. Easton Cottingham had been a larger-than-life figure, both in the Middle Chapel and in public affairs. He was on the Lincoln Board of Governors and in politics an ardent Liberal. He retired to Saxilby when his son took over the farm after he had suffered a stroke which left him partially paralysed, but he didn't give up, using a bath-chair to help him continue his activities.

His son Herbert Cottingham, who continued to farm at Broxholme, was an excellent singer, performing at numerous events and very active at the chapel. The family always tried to employ servants whose families were chapel people, like Clara Marshall, John Pacey and Lillian Ancliff.

William Dennis had moved to the village and set up as a chemist in the High Street. Both he and his wife Lizzie were regular attenders, with their children Leonard and Muriel going to Sunday School.

Herbert Sutcliffe, who took over Kirton's shop on Bridge Street and sold footwear and clothes to the village, was much involved in both the Sunday School and the Band of Hope.

John Charles, a Butcher, lived at `Riverdale' on Bridge Street, with his wife Elizabeth being in charge of the choir for many years.

James Hauton, who lived in Mays Lane and traded as a market gardener, was a stalwart member as well as organist, with his large family all attending Sunday School. His son Jack took over the family business as well as becoming a local preacher and much-loved leader of the Wesley Guild for many years; he is remembered with great affection

Joe Vasey was a local plumber who lived on Lincoln Road with his family. His elder daughter Connie (my mother) was very musical, singing in the choir and starting to play the organ. She became a Sunday School teacher, but also qualified as a primary school teacher at Derby College, taking up a post at Broadholme Primary School. Many of the children at the school attended the Sunday Schools at the chapels, so they knew 'Miss Vasey' very well. One lady who used to come into the post office regularly during the 1990s often talked to me about both Broadholme School and the Free Sunday School, telling me what an impact my mother had had on her early life.

Broadholme School about 1929/30

The Primitive Chapel

(now often known as the Bottom Chapel)

After the war membership at the Prims was on the decline, although stalwart families like that of Joseph Warrener from Hardwick and the Butler family were ever present, with their large families attending Sunday School.

Joseph Warrener and his wife Sarah had ten children in total, several of whom left the area choosing work in

Leicester as a coal dealer or grocer's assistant, but their youngest son John stayed local, marrying Lily and having two sons, Joseph Albert and John Henry *(known as Henry)* and a daughter Marjorie.

John Coulson Butler married Elmina Coulson from Kexby and they had one daughter Annie and three sons, Robert, Charles and John Henry *(known as Harry): see his memories below.* John died suddenly in 1922 and his widow married Joseph Askew and continued to be a staunch member at the Prims until it finally closed in 1943.

In 1941, Joseph Warrener's son Henry married John Coulson Butler's daughter Annie, having daughter Kathleen who married Ernie Hill from Thorney. Kathleen became a Sunday School teacher at the Godfrey Memorial chapel and their two sons attended Sunday School.

The widow of Bob Keyworth from Bedlam House, became a much respected member at the Prims, helping with all the events and public teas.

In February 1914 the congregation organised a twelve-day mission concluding with a 'providence tea' which was well attended and a large company was present at the evening meeting. The members were doing all they could to try to bring in more people.

Norman Valley recalls attending evening service at the Bottom chapel in the 1920s with one or two other young men, just to see what a hell-fire 'ranters' service was like. He was much reprimanded by his father, although he also recounted the wonderful 'stuffed chine supper' held there each Good Friday. It was a public tea open to all the village and was great money spinner for the chapel, but much distained by the Vicar who announced from his pulpit that parishioners should not attend.

Harry Butler recalls in great detail the excitement of these stuffed-chine suppers. His mother was in charge of preparing the *best and biggest 'neck chine'* from the pigs at Birchwood Farm and explains how it was cured and stuffed with parsley, onions and other spices, all mixed together in a big wooden chopping bowl and left to stand, before being stitched in to a large cloth before being boiled in a 60 gallon copper, situated in the wash-house and usually used for doing the laundry.

The local baker, Billy Redford, baked special bread and the ladies of the chapel, in their long black dresses, snow white aprons and flowered hats, served the public.

The special tea service used, black with gold edging and gold patterning, looking really imposing on the long tables covered in white linen, laid out ready for the 4pm start. It was a feast much enjoyed by many of the villagers who would be known to starve themselves in anticipation of this wonderful meal, which would cost one shilling per person.

When everyone was seated, the minister would announce that grace would be sung to the tune 'Old Hundredth' (All creatures that on earth do dwell) and Harry could still remember every word:-

Be present at our table lord, be here and everywhere adored,

Thy creatures bless and grant that we may feast in paradise with thee.

This 'stuffed chine tea' was obviously a grand event and has been recounted by numerous people, but it was Harry's mother, Elmina (Butler) Askew who told me all about it herself when I was a little girl, as she came to live in the cottage next door to Grayson's Stores, which was my home for many years. I was a regular visitor to her home, indeed sometimes staying the night there, when she would tell me tales about the village. When I began learning the piano, I loved playing the harmonium which she kept in her front room, finding it hard to pump the two large pedals in order to make it function. The Sunday School used to borrow this harmonium for the parade around the village as part of the Anniversary celebrations for many years, being heaved on to the front waggon using ropes and lots of helpers, with my mother pedalling away to lead the singing.

When the war was over the young men who survived returned to the village, but whilst some were happy to settle back into the familiarity of rural life, others were not content and expected something more. It was a subtle shift; with work now being available at the foundries in Lincoln there was movement to live in the town, whilst the village people began to turn their leisure time towards more sporting opportunities and enjoying the music and dancing of the 1920s. This in part was thanks to the Women's Institute purchasing and renovating an army hut from Thorney and erecting it in William Street; it proved to be an ideal venue for many community events. Whilst the congregations in all the chapels continued to prosper, with full Sunday Schools, more of the younger generations no longer felt they needed to attend on a regular basis.

It was also a time for questions to be asked about uniting the different branches of Methodism across the country. In Lincoln 1921 we know that important meetings began taking place under the title 'the breaking down of the middle wall' when ministers of the five Methodist circuits met to consider the idea of a one-and-undivided Methodist Church. Over the coming years, numerous meetings were held with joint committees pouring over proposals as to how the Union would work, with many grave predictions of serious conflict between the different tribes. Lincoln joint committee of Wesleyan-Primitive-United even issued a manifesto stating that the whole question should be postponed, but it was becoming inevitable that there would be a union at some point before too long.

Chapter 7

1932-1940: Uniting the chapels

It was the 20th September 1932 when all the different branches of Methodism finally came together at a Special Conference held in the Royal Albert Hall, London, to adopt the 'Deed of Union' after which the new united body would be known simply as 'The Methodist Church'. To distinguish it from Methodism in other countries, it was to be styled 'The Methodist Church of Great Britain'. There was to be a new Methodist hymn book, which would incorporate hymns from the different denominations, as well as some more modern hymns.

Now it was up to the three chapels in Saxilby to explore scenarios as to how unification would work in the village. As you can imagine it was not going to be straightforward, with three different 'tribes' trying to come together.

Obviously great compromises were going to be required and for a few people it would be extremely difficult. Whilst some local chapels were able to amalgamate quickly, it took Saxilby over ten years to finally worship together, and even then some members felt they could no longer attend a 'different' chapel and left.

How the people of the village knew 'which chapel was which' is difficult to imagine, but from the date of the union in 1932, when the familiar names of Primitives, UMFC (Frees) and Wesleyans disappeared, the chapels became known locally as 'High Street Chapel' 'Central Chapel' and 'Top Chapel'. Things were further complicated because as we know, the different branches of Methodism all used the same idea of grouping churches together in what was known as a circuit, and after 1932, the Top Chapel remained in the Lincoln Wesley Circuit, whereas the Central Chapel and the High Street Chapel both became part of the new Trinity Circuit. The circuit matter was a critical issue for amalgamating the three chapels in Saxilby, and it took a number of years for it to be finally resolved.

During the ensuing years the chapels continued to have their own regular services, the Anniversary events went ahead in each church and the Sunday schools continued successfully, but from 1932 when everyone was under the same governance, they did begin to work together. We learn from the Lincolnshire Echo in November 1935 that there was a weekend rally of Methodists at Saxilby, incorporating all three chapels.

On the Saturday there was a 'welcome meeting' and 'song service' held in the former Primitive Methodist Chapel with Mr F. Strapps of Lincoln conducting the singing. A special visiting preacher from Romford, the Rev George H Simpson, took the Sunday services both morning and evening at the Wesleyan Chapel, with a service for the children in the afternoon. On the Monday there was an afternoon service at the Central Chapel (ex-Frees) followed by a providence tea which was well attended. Rev Simpson gave a lecture in the evening, supported by Ministers from the different circuits.

Fund-raising events continued to ensure that there were funds available to keep all the chapels running, and garden fetes were always a popular way of raising money, with the Lang family hosting numerous such events at their home, Rose Villa, over the years, but after Dick Lang's wife Mary Helen died very suddenly in 1931, Albert Little and his wife Ada offered their garden at Ingleby Hall for future events and these became an annual attraction as well as an excellent way of raising funds.

Albert Little was a farmer at Ingleby and the family had always attended the Wesleyan Chapel, but over the years they became good friends with the Vasey family who worshipped at the Free Chapel, with their children sharing many pastimes – playing tennis, singing and all becoming Sunday School teachers. Integration between families helped enormously as the chapels started to work together. Regrettably, the Little's only daughter Mary suffered from poor health and following the death of her mother, became a semi-invalid. I often accompanied my mother, who visited her regularly, and remember feeling very sad for her laid in a bed downstairs at the Hall, with beautiful views out across the fields, but never able to go out and about.

Other members also took their turn in hosting such enjoyable events with Mr & Mrs Francis Clark arranging a garden party in 1934 in the grounds of their home, known as 'The Pastures', where they raised the sum of £18 for chapel and Sunday School funds. The main attractions at these events was 'bowling for a pig' and 'skittling for a pig', hoopla stalls and various other competitions. There was always a magnificent tea available, usually followed in the evening with a concert or other musical entertainment.

Mr Clark was a teacher at the boys' grammar school in Lincoln, whilst his wife Hilda Clark became a County Councillor for many years. They raised a large family, with their eldest daughter Marjorie marrying Geoff Ford and becoming a much-respected teacher at Saxilby school, and one of their sons, Michael, becoming a Methodist Minister. Their grandson David lives in Walnut House in the village, built by Geoff's father in 1906.

Mrs Clark was awarded a certificate from the Royal Humane Society for rescuing her grand-daughters Jennifer and Stephanie when the pony and trap they were all riding in became caught on the bank and capsized into the Fossdyke. Mrs Clark had leaped out to try to get hold of the pony's head, but the trap was dragged into the canal and completely submerged in the water, so she immediately plunged into the canal fully clothed and was able to get hold of both children and bring them to the bank.

The family were greatly involved in the struggle for social justice, both in the local community and beyond, and when the Jarrow marchers passed through the county in 1936, they offered sustenance as well as their field for the men to camp in overnight as they made their way to London carrying a petition to the government requesting the re-establishment of industry in the town following the closure of its main employer, Palmer's shipyard. Whilst the march produced few immediate results, over the subsequent years the Jarrow March became recognised by historians as a defining event of the 1930s.

As well as singing at chapel on a Sunday, there were numerous concerts and musical performances going on around the county during this period which my mother, Connie Vasey, was much involved in. As well as being a Sunday School teacher, she played the organ at the Free Chapel and led the choir, which had already gained a reputation for bringing high-class music into village life. Oratorios like The Messiah (Handel), The Creation (Haydn) or Elijah (Mendelssohn) were regularly performed at the large chapels in Lincoln, Gainsborough, Kirton Lindsey and Grantham. There were annual music festivals and competitions in Lincoln, Cleethorpes, Scunthorpe and North Lincolnshire, with Grantham & District holding an Eisteddfod. It was at the Grand Finalists Concert of the

Eisteddfod in 1937 when my mother shared a stage with a young Methodist girl named Margaret Roberts, who had received a Gold Medal for her recitation of 'Silver' by Walter De La Mare. The young girl went on to be the UK's first female prime minister, Margaret Thatcher.

There had been a Choral Society in Saxilby for many years, performing concerts and cantatas to packed audiences. After the war they could now meet in the W.I. Hut with members drawn from chapel and church and in 1934 a concert took place to raise money for the society featuring the Lincoln Orchestra, with solos by Miss Connie Vasey, Miss Dorothy Keall, Mr Joe Vasey and Mr Booth (from Lincoln Cathedral), accompanied by Miss Kathy Lang. Later that year, the three choirs of Saxilby, Scampton & Sturton Choral Societies joined together under the 'Lindsey Joint Village Choral scheme' and gave a concert in the Sturton Village Institute conducted by Mr Elsmere of Burton-by-Lincoln, which the Lincolnshire Chronicle described as 'magnificent'. The main item on the programme was 'The May Queen' by Sterndale Bennett, sung by over sixty choristers, plus an orchestra of sixteen. The quality of the performance was described as excellent, especially being arranged in a village!

As the years went on, the Wesleyans and the Frees, who had already worked together on various occasions and knew each other well, made plans to amalgamate in the short term, but to build a new chapel in the future which would unite all three branches in the village. The big question was, who would be willing to give up their chapel? The Wesleyans felt their chapel was where Methodism began, but the Free Chapel was superior in structure, so after much deliberation and with Mr Dick Lang driving the concept of unification, the Trustees of the 'Central Chapel' agreed they should amalgamate with the 'Top Chapel', but with the firm intention of uniting in a new chapel as soon as possible. The next question was, who would be willing to buy such a large building without proper heating and lighting?

It was a known fact within the village that various efforts had been made over many years to provide Saxilby with a village hall, even as far back as 1910 there had been a committee formed to consider the best method of providing a hall. Mr Dickerson Lang reported to the Parish Council that they had drawn up two schemes to be considered. The first scheme comprised a brick building with a second storey, costing £510. The second scheme was for a single storey iron building which would cost £375. Yet no scheme had ever been realised, and of course the costs of building kept rising. However, in 1929 retired farmer, William Watmough, left a legacy of £800 to help provide a village hall for Saxilby, with the stipulation that the project had to be completed within ten years. Obviously that provision was put into his will because he knew of the many aborted attempts over the past years. The Chapel Trustees, led by Mr Lang, were aware of the fruitless years searching for either a plot of land on which to build a new village hall or a suitable building to convert, so early in 1936 they approached the Parish Council to enquire if they would be interested in buying the chapel as a village hall.

The negotiations carried on for many months before arriving at a final decision and in the meantime the chapel continued with its normal programme of worship and special events, with a Sacred Concert taking place in April, a very successful garden party and concert at Rose Villa in June and the Sunday School Anniversary in July, with harvest celebrations in September. It must have been a difficult time for the chapel, anticipating they could soon close, yet still finding the enthusiasm to carry on as normal.

Meanwhile at the Parish Council meeting of 27th March 1936 discussions centred on the offer of purchasing the Central Chapel. It was decided to form a sub-committee, employing valuers and experts to ascertain the cost of a suitable hall, either new or reconditioned. By July the Parish Meeting were presented with estimates for both a new hall of adequate size, or the cost of the chapel with alterations. The meeting voted in favour of purchasing the Central Chapel and after some negotiation agreed to pay the sum of £650 for the building and the land. The initial £800 from Mr Watmough had gained interest in the intervening years and by now had grown to about £1000, so there was enough money left over from the purchase to install heating and electric lighting and it was hoped to spend a further amount removing the roof of the old schoolroom and building a reading room, billiard room and cloakroom on the upper level. It took until the end of October for the architect to draw up plans for two different schemes, which then had to be costed and examined, but finally late in 1936 the sale was completed. The last service took place at the chapel on Sunday 3rd January 1937 and by November that same year the main part of the village hall was officially opened by Mr C F Shaw, Chairman of the Parish Council.

The first amalgamated service at the Wesleyan Chapel was on Sunday 10th January 1937 and immediately a fund was started to build a new place of worship as a fresh start for all the denominations to come together. It was quite a task, even though they had the proceeds from the sale of the central chapel, but it was greatly assisted by a legacy from one of the chapel's oldest members, Mr George Godfrey, who passed away on 19th November 1937 leaving the sum of £1500 for the building of a new chapel. Rather like Mr Watmough, he added the proviso that the work must start within two years of his death, as he was aware how long such schemes take to finally reach conclusion. He also requested that the Chapel should be named 'The Godfrey Memorial Methodist Church'.

Meanwhile the life of the newly amalgamated chapels carried on, as they endeavoured to overcome the many difficulties of worshipping together. Remember the original divisions had been about governance, and now we have the Free Methodists giving up their own chapel where they had worshipped so freely, moving into the Wesleyan chapel, which had a much more regulated framework.

A good example of this was discovered in the Archives, when reading pages of the many different minute books of meetings of the Wesleyan Chapel compared to the Free Chapel who had just one book, containing all the happenings in the chapel over a period of 35 years.

The problems of both chapels still being in different circuits was also an obstacle, with each chapel continuing to have its own dedicated Ministers. Not ideal, but I think Saxilby was most fortunate to have Mr Dick Lang as someone willing to lead the amalgamation because he was visionary about the benefits of being united, determined to make the transition work as smoothly and optimistically as possible. The Primitives, although starting to work more closely with the other chapels, made no attempt to move to the Wesleyan Chapel, waiting until the new chapel had been opened and was seen to be working well. Meanwhile the Jackson organ had to be moved from the Free Chapel to the Wesley Chapel, only to be moved again when the new chapel was built.

We know from old minute books that the first '*United*' *Sunday School* met on Sunday January 10th 1937, but prior to that there had already been a Teachers Meeting in December 1936 to work out how the classes would function and who would be in charge of the different age groups. We also learn that the Free Methodist Sunday School had many more children than the Wesleyans, in the Primary Department, the ex-Free children made up 75% of the numbers, and in general were much more financially secure. Compromise was arrived at by making joint-Sunday School Superintendents and mixing the teachers into different classes.

It was agreed the joint Superintendents for the Junior/Senior Departments would be Mr G T Day (ex-Wesleyan) and Mr D Lang (ex-Frees), each to take alternate Sunday services. Miss H Day (ex-Wesleyan) and Miss K Lang (ex-Frees) were elected as Joint Superintendents of the Primary Department.

The question of song books wasn't straightforward either, as the ex-United Sunday School had been using the Cary Bonner hymnal, but it agreed to buy the new Methodist Sunday School hymn book for the older children which would be used going forward, and new Cary Bonner 'print only' books would be purchased for the Primary children. There would be a morning Sunday School from 10am–10.25am with Mr Dick Lang taking charge and Miss May Franklin elected pianist. The afternoon session would begin at two o'clock and finish at 2.45, each class to have its own register.

The Sunday School Anniversary weekend was permanently fixed for the second Sunday in June every year, with a parade around the village on the Monday afternoon. (We also learn from the Minute book that the School Managers were requested each year to close the school for the afternoon!)

At the next meeting held on 19th February 1937, the Treasurer's report was given, showing that the sum of

£5.14s.10d had been transferred from the ex-United funds and 7s.2d from the ex-Wesleyan funds, making a total to commence the year of £6.2s.

Arrangements for the Sunday School Anniversary were discussed at length. Mr Harold Acliff (farmer at Broadholme) would be asked to provide seven drays which would be needed to accommodate the much-enlarged combined Sunday School children for their parade around the village during the afternoon, and Mr Brown to loan his field for the sports/games.

Two new teachers were approved – Miss Barbara Keall for the Big School and Mrs Ivy Rowlands to help in the Primary. Mr Jim Read was elected Auditor for the Treasurer's books.

And so the first United Sunday School Anniversary took place on 15th June 1937 with a similar event held in June 1938, following the pattern both chapels had used for decades, with special performances by the children in the afternoon and parading round the village on the Monday, followed by sports in Mr Brown's field.

However, it appears not all was going smoothly between some members of the Sunday School staff, and at the meeting held in November 1938 we learn that the 'rather antagonistic feeling between certain of the teachers' needed to be addressed! The Rev. Thomas attended the meeting and appealed to them all to make a new start in the spirit of Christian co-operation. It seems the Wesley Sunday School had always had rather strict rules for their children to follow and had decided that similar rules should govern the new United Sunday School, which had not gone down well with a number of children from the Free Chapel, with attendances starting to decrease. The situation only improved when the new chapel was open and certain teachers from the Sunday School moved away.

Chapel Anniversaries were held in the Top Chapel, but the difficulties of having members from two circuits needed to be resolved and in June 1938 discussions began regarding suggested schemes for circuit amalgamation. It was accepted that changes to prevent unnecessary overlapping in the villages were practicable, but any immediate attempt to form a new circuit would sever the long connection between Wesley and so many churches south of the river – again there is the inference that the ex-Wesley churches are more important than the other societies. It wasn't until September 1944 that proposals for the amalgamation of circuits finally came to fruition, although it took a further two years for the new Aldersgate Circuit, incorporating 48 churches, to come into full effect.

Harvest Festival celebrations were easier to arrange because both chapels had arranged their celebrations in much the same way, so the 'Top United Chapel' was decorated in the usual festive way, with sheaves of corn, lots of flowers, fruit and vegetables. The High Street Chapel (ex-Prims) still held their own festival, but as the Lincolnshire Echo reported in 1938, they now had an ex-Wesleyan local preacher, Mr G W Abbott from Langworth, taking the services. At the Monday night meeting Mr W H Keyworth from the ex-Free Chapel presided and music was provided by Mr Tom Strapps of Lincoln with Miss Kathy Lang (ex-Free) on the piano. It appeared the unification of the Methodist Church was gradually beginning to shows signs of working as it was intended, although members from the Frees always referred to it as an amalgamation, only being united when the new chapel was built.

Because of the two-year clause in Mr Godfrey's bequest, it was critical that work should start on a new chapel. Special efforts had to be made to find a suitable site and draw up plans to do so within the time-frame, as well as raise the extra cash which would be required to build a suitable chapel that would stand the test of time. Fortunately the field across the road from the Top Chapel was identified as ideal and in May 1938 a deposit of £28 was paid for the purchase of land from Mr W H Smith, but it wasn't until 8th July 1939 that plans were fully approved and building could commence.

Fund-raising events were quickly underway to raise funds to help pay for the new building, not least because monies from the normal Sunday collections and special services were allocated to the routine upkeep of the chapel. As you can see, a number of events were organised, but unfortunately the amounts raised were not large:-

On Wednesday 2nd February 1939 the Rev. E W Pape of Ockbrook in Derbyshire paid a special visit to the 'Top Methodist Church' to give a lecture entitled 'Some Famous Hymns and Authors' followed by a public tea. In the evening Rev Pape gave a story-recital called 'Jamie Somer, Humourist and Cynic'. The sum of £5 was raised from the event.

Later the same month, on Sunday/Monday 12th/13th February, special centenary services were held at the 'Top Methodist Chapel'. The Rev G H Simpson travelled from Brighton to take the services. He stayed on to attend a community singing event on the Monday afternoon and after the usual public tea, gave a presentation in the evening. Proceeds from the entire weekend came to just over £13, which all went to the new chapel fund.

On Wednesday 15th March there was a bazaar held in the village hall, organised by ladies of the chapel. Mrs John Jay of Lincoln opened the event, when she was presented with a bouquet by Patricia Grayson. A comic operetta was staged later on by the Junior Choir of the Lincolnshire Co-operative Education Committee.

Over the weekends of 21st/28th April, the men of the chapel organised a variety of efforts totalling over £18 for the new building fund.

Although these events contributed towards the new building fund, it was going to take a long time to reach the amount necessary to build the new chapel, and of course time was not on their side. Mr Godfrey's bequest was quite clear that the building must commence within two years of his death and although a site was purchased quite quickly, getting the plans drawn up and approved proved quite protracted, especially as the Methodist General Chapel

Committee in Manchester had to be involved.

Even as late as May 1939, the General Secretary from Manchester was in correspondence, expressing grave concern about the money available to build the new chapel according to the plans which had been submitted. They were also concerned about the design and structure of the roof and the lavatory accommodation and extremely anxious about the provision made for the Sunday School - in their opinion it was totally inadequate and alternative plans must be drawn up. In June, architects agreed to make the chapel smaller by cutting out the transept and having just one vestry. They also agreed to put in an extra lavatory (would you believe the gentlemen had no toilet provisions in the original plan) but it wasn't until the 5th July that permission was finally given by the General Chapel Committee, and only on condition that the old chapel must not be sold until provision for extra Sunday School accommodation be found, as until then the old chapel could be used as required.

And so the stone-laying ceremony planned for the following weekend was allowed to go ahead, described in some detail by the Lincolnshire Chronicle.

On the weekend of 11th/12th July, the stone-laying ceremony took place, just four months before the time laid down by Mr George Geoffrey expired. There was a service in the Top Chapel with ministers from both circuits taking part. The Rev William Selby (from the Wesley circuit) gave the address, expressing his delight with the way members from both chapels were working together. The Rev John Jay (from the Trinity circuit) gave a dedicatory prayer. The congregation then adjourned to the site of the new chapel immediately opposite the present building.

There the commemorative stones were laid. Mrs Brown, of Sturton-by-Stow and formerly of Saxilby, laid the first stone in memory of Mr George Godfrey, her half cousin, whose bequest had made the scheme possible. Mrs Brown was presented with a silver trowel.

Stone-laying for the new Methodist Chapel, July 1939

Ten other stones were laid by the following:

Mr A. Tear (in memory of the late Mrs Tear)

Miss White

Mr & Mrs D. Lang (2 stones)

Mr C Credland (in memory of the late Mr George Credland)

Mr & Miss Hotchkin (2 stones)

Mr G. Smalley

Mr J Whittles (in memory of the late Mr William Whittles)

Mr Martin Drury (in memory of the late Mr William Drury)

Twenty-eight bricks were also laid at a donation of 5/- each. A public tea was laid on with a public meeting in the chapel with both ministers and local preachers giving addresses. A grand sum of £35 was raised for the new building fund.

Following the stone-laying ceremony in July, the building of the new chapel commenced and as my grandfather, Joseph W Vasey was the treasurer, I've been lucky to come across the account book, giving details of the many companies involved:

Messrs Danby Epton & Griffiths
Solicitors acting for sale of UMC

Mr W H Smith
Sale of land

Messrs Andrew Race & Co.
Solicitors acting for new building

Messrs Crouch, Butler & Savage
Architects of Birmingham

Wm Wright & Son Ltd of Lincoln
Builders

Herbert Hardy of Saxilby
Fencing

Cousans of Lincoln
Organ moving/installation

Mawer & Collingham of Lincoln
Carpets & mats

Messrs Wall Bros Ltd.
Seating

There was a tremendous amount of work involved in building the new chapel, whilst keeping the newly amalgamated 'Top Chapel' operating as smoothly as possible. Fund-raising continued as a matter of urgency because there was a shortfall in funds, as had been predicted by the General Chapel Committee, but they did agree to allow a temporary debt in order to get the building completed. Stage payments were arranged with most of the contractors, which helped, but as the date of completion drew near it was apparent there was urgent need for about £300. Fortunately six people were in a position to lend £50 each and thanks were expressed to the following people for their willingness to assist in allowing the completion to go ahead on schedule.

- Mr Richard N Hauton
- Mr Bert Hotchkin
- Mr Dickerson Lang
- Mr Albert Little
- Mr Percy Smalley and
- Mr Joseph W Vasey

Even as the work was proceeding, on Sunday 3rd September 1939 at 11.15 in the morning, Prime Minister Neville Chamberlain announced that the country was now at war, which added yet more stress to try to get the building finished before materials dried up as the country prepared for what was to come. In fact, many of the issues which came to light over the years with the building, especially the roof, stemmed from the fact that materials used were not of the quality they should have been.

GODFREY MEMORIAL METHODIST CHURCH
Building Account: March1937-Nov 1940

Income		Expenditure	
Sale of UMFC	650.00	Purchase of land	281.00
Trust cash from UMFC	39.00	Solicitors/search fees	13.00
Exors: George Godfrey	1500.00	Fencing	11.00
Donations & Subscriptions	150.00	Builders	2335.00
Stone-laying ceremony	108.00	Architects	81.00
Money-raising events	150.00	Organ move/installation	13.00
Bank Interest	65.00	Carpets & Mats	7.00
Loans to cover shortfall	*300.00*	Seating	220.00
TOTAL:	**2962.00**	**TOTAL:**	**2962.00**

On the 21st March 1940 the new Godfrey Memorial Methodist Church held its first service, with a packed congregation, but it took another four years before the Primitives finally closed their chapel and united at the Godfrey Memorial Church.

My grandfather donated a stained glass window for the back of the chapel, above the choir stalls, with the inscription: *'In gratitude to God – presented by Joseph W and Minnie K Vasey and their daughters Connie and Gladys'*

For many years after the closure of the Primitive Chapel, a group of older ladies would still meet in a room at their old chapel once a week, thanks to the generosity of Mr Richard Hauton, who leased the Primitive Chapel for his Market Garden business. The group was called the 'Bright Hour' and I remember asking the question 'why is it called the Bright Hour when all the ladies wear black?' Of course most of them were widows and it was still the tradition for them to continue wearing black! Kathleen Hill tells me that she and her cousin Christine Gibson would often attend these afternoon occasions with their grandmother Mrs Elmina Askew, being advised to 'sit still and keep quiet', but the other ladies would say 'just let the bairns sing', and so they did. Happy memories today of times long past.

Chapter 8

1940-1952: Settling in at the New Chapel

The country was already at war by the time the new chapel was opened and very quickly Saxilby found itself surrounded by airfields as the area's flat geography lent itself to runways and airstrips, in fact Lincolnshire became known as 'Bomber County'. It's difficult to comprehend just how many RAF squadrons were stationed in the area during the years of the war, but most were bomber stations: Dunholme Lodge, Faldingworth, Fiskerton, Hemswell, Ingham, Skellingthorpe, Swinderby, Wigsley, and of course the famous Scampton airfield, home to 617 squadron, who became known as 'The Dam Busters'. The sound of these huge planes flying in vast numbers over the village would have been deafening as well as fearsome, with Manchesters, Wellingtons and finally Lancasters being operational during the course of the conflict. My parents often talked about how they would count the planes as they set out on their night's mission and anxiously count the numbers returning in the early morning. It must have been incredibly upsetting to realise when planes were missing.

The Saxilby History Group have written about the impact of the war on the village in their book 'Step Back in Time', including the formation of the Home Guard, the Observer Corps and the Fire Service, involving most of the local men who were unable to join up for various reasons but reading the in-depth account of these organisations, the impact on the village becomes obvious. The many adaptations necessary in keeping the country functioning during the war years, meant that life was turned upside down for so many families and would never return to how it was before.

The recently vacated ex-Wesleyan Centenary Chapel was soon helping the war effort, as a division of the Scottish Horse Artillery moved into the village and both the chapel and the village hall were in use accommodating the soldiers. Individual householders who had spare rooms volunteered to help and my own parents, newly-wed and living in William Street, had two people stay with them. They were still in touch with the men and their families after the war and as a little girl remember one couple coming to stay, they spoke with such a strong Scottish accent, I found it hard to understand them. They were reminiscing about evenings spent round the piano at Winston House, singing community hymns and songs and how it kept their spirits high during such a dreadful time.

The newly opened Godfrey Memorial Methodist Church continued with regular services and anniversaries throughout the war, which were important to help keep life as normal as possible both for the children and the villagers, giving them the opportunity to come together as the 'family of the church' to strengthen their faith in such troubling times. Many of the concerts and other events held during these years of conflict raised money for various funds connected with the war effort.

Photo shows the inside of the new Godfrey Memorial Chapel with its dark beams. The photo was possibly taken at a children's event as many of the hymns on the notice board are from the children's section and look to be accompanied by the piano rather than the organ.

Many weddings took place during this period, often arranged at short notice, as young men serving in the forces managed to get leave. My own parents, Connie Vasey and John Rawson, were the first couple to be married in the 'New Methodist Chapel' as it was often referred to (rather than the Godfrey Memorial as the bequest stated!) The chapel officially opened on 21st March and on the Easter Monday, 25th March, their wedding took place, with the reception in the school room.

There was some last-minute stress as to whether the wedding could take place, as the question of the Marriage Register was in doubt. At the end of February 1940, the General Register Office in Blackpool sent a letter stating: 'whilst willing for the new building to be registered for marriages in substitution for the old, it would be necessary for the Office to receive a plan of the lay-out of the new church, accompanied by a completed Worship Certificate, before they could grant a substitution of the Register'. There was only a month for this to happen and when advised there was a wedding planned for 25th March, replied stating 'the marriage may not be lawfully solemnised until the Register had been authorised, and it would have to take place in the old building.' Fortunately for my parents, the necessary paperwork was received in time!

Whether there were any seats for guests to sit at during the wedding I honestly don't know, as it appeared there was a delay in the seats arriving, due mainly to the workmen being called-up. Even when they were completed, the wire-rack underneath each seat was missing as by this time the factory had been taken over by the Government. There was also a disagreement on whether there should be a central aisle (with seating either side) as proposed by the Trustees or two side-aisles (with block of twelve seats in the middle) as drawn up in the official plans agreed by Manchester. For those who have attended the chapel will know, the Trustees won the argument: there was indeed a central aisle, but this explains the conundrum of why there were two doors at the front of the building, one of which was never used! On the scheme of things, the fact that the chapel was completed under wartime conditions was a great achievement. Even the General Secretary of the Methodist General Committee at Manchester sent a congratulatory letter, expressing his delight that the new chapel was now open for worship.

Having been brought up within the family of the Free Methodist Chapel, attending Sunday School, singing in the choir, becoming organist at a very young age, teaching in the Sunday School and finally taking over the choir, my mother was delighted to be the first to be married in the 'New Methodist Church' and felt that it was home to her for the rest of her life, devoting herself to creating music and singing for the joy of all. She played the organ for numerous weddings during her time at the chapel, she lost count of how many, but never took any money as virtually all the many people who have been married at the chapel had come through the Sunday School or had been baptised there, so she knew them all.

Wedding of the author's parents, Connie & John Rawson, 25th March 1940

As you can see from the photo, my mother had been able to acquire a very elegant lace dress, but as the years of hardship went on, rationing meant that clothing was extremely difficult to acquire, and in later years dress fabric had to be procured from a variety of sources, including parachutes.

The problems of the combined chapels still retaining their own circuits continued to bring complications, even though the ex-Wesleyans and the ex-Frees were all now worshipping together in their new chapel. It took until 1944 for the difficulties to be fully resolved when a new circuit, named 'Lincoln Aldersgate Circuit', came into being. It was at this point that the Primitive Methodists eventually closed their chapel in the village and joined the Godfrey Memorial Church, finally making the new chapel fully united in worship, with all three societies of Methodism coming together.

I think perhaps here would be a good place to explore the importance of how the new Methodist Church was to be governed. Bearing in mind it was this subject which had caused the splits only a century earlier. The structures now required for an organisation the size of Methodism to be managed can be seen in the diagram on the next page. It gives the different tiers of management and indicates how every member is supported and feels part of the whole by the overarching role of the Connexion.

Conference

Conference set the ruling framework and had always ensured that gambling of every kind was expressly forbidden on all Methodist premises or for the raising of funds, including raffles, games of chance, sweepstakes, guessing and other competitions which involve the principle of the raffle. No entertainment could be given on Church premises without the programme being approved by the Minister and also directed that the wine used for the Sacrament of the Lord's supper must be unfermented.

Districts

Districts were spread out across the country and were the

first level after Conference to give direction and support to the circuits and work alongside the Connexion.

STRUCTURE of the METHODIST CHURCH

CONFERENCE
President & Vice President elected annually
*supported by The Methodist Council
and Connexional Committee*

DISTRICTS
led by District Chair
*supported by District Synod (Assembly)
providing link between Conference, Connexional Team & Circuits*

CIRCUITS
group of Churches with team of Ministers
led by Superintendent Minister
*supported by voluntary circuit stewards
responsible for direction and policy of the Circuit*

LOCAL CHURCHES
led by volunteers known as stewards
*congregations based on the original 'society'
who manage their own affairs*

THE CONNEXION
All Methodists are part of a larger connected
community known as the Connexion which in turn
feeds into the Conference

Circuits

There were often a sizeable number of circuits in each District led by a Superintendent Minister with responsibility for the local churches attached to each circuit, having to complete a preaching plan each quarter and pay to have it printed and distributed. This ensured each chapel knew who would be taking their services for coming weeks.

The number of officials and committees to support a circuit the size of the new Lincoln Aldersgate Circuit was substantial. It had six appointed Ministers, each being attached to one main church (listed below)

1. Hannah Memorial
2. Portland Place
3. Rasen Lane & Saxon Street
4. St. Catherines
5. Moorland Park
6. Saxilby *(There had never been a minister live outside the city before and this obviously reflected the large membership and the healthy finances of Godfrey Memorial now it had a united congregation)*

The income of the circuit came from levying an amount based on the numbers of registered members at each chapel, whereby an 'assessment' was charged, which had to be paid every quarter.

Sections

The Circuit then apportioned main churches into sections, with each Minister being responsible for a number of smaller local churches.

Saxilby section at this time included Skellingthorpe, Harby, Sturton-by-Stow, North Scarle (High Street), North Scarle (North End), Spalford and Scampton.

The main church of Aldersgate Circuit was Hannah

Memorial, the big imposing building on the High Street, with an upper gallery, which meant it could accommodate sectional gatherings. It was also the hub for Circuit Festivals which took place each year and other large events.

Local Churches

Each Church then had to appoint people to the following positions to ensure the Society was correctly managed:

- Trustees, who had considerable responsibility to hold the property in Trust for the Methodist people and to ensure that worship at the chapel was in accordance with the rules from Conference.

- Society Stewards, who were appointed by the Leaders' Meeting, which was in overall charge of the working of the chapel as a whole. They were responsible for making payments on behalf of the Society and for attending Circuit Meetings.

- Poor Fund Stewards, again appointed annually by the Leaders' Meeting to ensure the sacrament was appropriately managed, including the collection taken as well as distributing monies to those in need within the society.

- Chapel Stewards, who were appointed by the Trustees' Meeting to look after the fabric and furniture of the premises, ensuring they were in good repair and clean.

- Every quarter the leaders of all the different organisations within the chapel, came together to ensure everyone was included in what was happening. This was known as the 'Leaders' Meeting'.

The first Minister to be appointed to Saxilby in August 1946 was the Rev. J. W. Lamb (known as 'Woolly' by the young people) who originated from Newcastle. He had spent 13 years in London becoming a Minister in the Forest Gate Circuit, before serving as an Army Chaplain for six years during the war. There was no manse for him to live in, so initially he moved into Rose Villa, the home of Mr Dick Lang, who no doubt was of great assistance to him in his early years, later moving into the centre of the village, lodging with Miss Bemrose in South Parade. He replaced the Rev John Jay, who had been overseeing Saxilby during the transition, and became a supernumerary Minister for the Aldersgate Circuit, continuing to live in West Parade, Lincoln.

At a Trustees' meeting in April 1947 the idea of purchasing a Manse in Saxilby was discussed, and as Mr Joe Vasey suggested a suitable house might be offered for sale in the near future, it was agreed to form a sub-committee to look into this proposal. By September the Circuit had agreed to purchase the property, but several Circuit members were added to the Saxilby Trustees to form an official Manse Committee as the purchase of a property at 40 Church Road, known as 'Homelea' went ahead. The Trustees were most grateful to Philip Race, who was a solicitor at the firm of Andrew, Race, Midgeley & Hill in Lincoln, as he did all the legal work without charging a fee. He came from a prominent Methodist family who were all active in the life of the Methodist movement in the area. His brother Steve Race went on to be a composer, pianist and radio and television presenter. He is probably best remembered as the chairman of the light-hearted radio and TV panel game 'My Music', which ran from 1967 to 1994.

It appears that the Rev Lamb was not particularly well-regarded by many of the congregation and according to anecdotal records, his sermons 'went on forever'. On one particular occasion he was remembered as turning round to look at the choir members (who sat behind the pulpit facing the congregation) just as one lady was looking at her watch, and told her in a stern loud voice 'I'm not finished yet'. He only stayed for two years before the Rev John Earl arrived in September 1948. The Rev Earl soon fitted into village life and was well liked by everyone. His wife Kitty joined the ladies' group as well as becoming a teacher in the Sunday School, whilst daughter Leila attended the Girls High School in Lincoln along with several girls from the Sunday School.

As Rev Earl arrived, the following people were currently in role to help and assist him and ensure the chapel prospered:

- Society Stewards: Messrs Dick Lang, Joe Pacey, John Mayfield and Jim Whittles

- Chapel Stewards: Messrs Tom Day, Bob Talks, Herbert Valley and Ernest James

- Poor Stewards: Mr William Long and Mrs Martin Drury

- Leaders' Meeting: Secretary – Mr William Long

- Trustees   Secretary – Mr Joe Valley

- Treasurer: Mr Tom Day

- Choirmaster: Mrs John Rawson
  Assistant: Mr William Long

- Organists: Mesdames J Rawson, J Valley,
  F Ford and Mr Donald Valley

- Sunday School: Superintendents - Mesdames D Lang,
  R Talks, M Turner & G T Day
  Secretary/Treasurer– Messrs Donald &
  Bernard Valley

- Guild: Secretary – Mr Jack Hauton
  Treasurer – Miss Hilda Hotchkin

- Women's Meeting: Secretary – Mrs C Credland
  Treasurer – Mrs J Whittles

Obviously the four Society Stewards ensured the chapel operated in accordance with the rulings of Conference: Mr Dick Lang from the Free Chapel, Mr Joe Pacey and Mr Jim Whittles from the Wesley Chapel and Mr James Mayfield from the Primitive Chapel, thus ensuring that even after being united in 1932, all sections of the movement were still equally involved in the management of the chapel almost twenty years later. Dick Lang was the son of the Methodist Minister who came to Lincoln to work as part of the United Methodist Free Church. We already know his story from previous chapters as he'd been the driving force at the Free

Chapel for many years and had played a pivotal role in the amalgamation of the Wesleyans and the Frees in 1936/7.

Joe Pacey had lived and worked at Manor Farm (opposite the entrance to the Parish Church in Church Lane) with his wife and two daughters Gwen and Gill. When Mr Pacey retired, the family moved to a bungalow at the top of Church Road and it was there he fulfilled one of his many obligations as Senior Society Steward, having a meal prepared for the new Minister and family when they moved into the Manse at Homelea, which was just across the road. Gill tells me they always became friends with the Minister's family and she can recall stories in vivid detail about the many children who lived there. Her father was always a great advocate of being involved in the Circuit, seeing the wider picture thereby ensuring the Chapel in Saxilby didn't become insular and inward looking. When his wife died, Gill had to take over many of the roles her mother had fulfilled, including organising a tea in the Village Hall for a Circuit Quarterly Meeting held in Saxilby, no mean feat for someone aged only 19.

Jim Whittles had been an agnostic in his youth and even when he married Jessima Credland, the daughter of a prominent Wesleyan Methodist in Saxilby in 1914, he never attended services or had anything to do with the chapel. They lived near the family home in Church Lane and he started a business selling Calor gas. According to the recollection of Norman Valley, some years later *he became extremely ill with pneumonia and was rushed into hospital at death's door, but he survived and from that moment on he asked for his sins to be forgiven and he became a Christian.* Indeed for many years he played a huge role in the chapel, becoming a Circuit Steward as well as Chapel Steward.

James Mayfield worked on a farm all his life, marrying Mary Jane Dove from Saxilby at the turn of the century. Their first home was at Gate Burton, where their family of three sons and one daughter were born, before moving to Broadholme, where he was in charge of the horses. He then moved to Church Farm in Church Lane before retiring to live down Mays Lane. He is fondly remembered always carrying his raincoat over his arm – apparently he never went anywhere without it.

Joe Pacey on Guild trip with Elsie Foster, Gill Pacey, Ethel Walker, Alma Hauton and Mary Gelder

One of the first things Rev Earl initiated was the setting up of a group for young people aged 14 and over, with the aim of keeping the older Sunday School members involved in the life of the chapel. Initially it was called the 'Young People's' Church' and started in January 1949 with my mother Connie Rawson as leader and Roy Hauton assisting, soon becoming known as the 'Junior Church'. When Roy left a couple of years later, his cousin Jack Hauton became involved and together Connie and Jack nurtured a group of young people who were very active in the chapel and became well-known in the neighbouring villages as they would go out as a group, taking services in all the smaller chapels in the area.

The Hauton family had been members of the Free Chapel for over 50 years, with James Hauton and his wife Ellen moving to Saxilby to set up a gardening business, they went on to have five children, although their youngest son George died in 1926. Eldest son Richard Newell Hauton worked for the family's market garden in the village, marrying Gladys Robson and had just one son Jack. It was Richard who purchased the old Primitive Chapel.

His son Jack married Alma Long, daughter of a Wesleyan local preacher who lived in William Street and although they never had a family of their own, they worshipped at the Godfrey Memorial Chapel all their lives, with Jack being a well-regarded local preacher as well as the leader of the Guild for many years. Second son Alfred Martin Hauton also worked in the business and married local girl Ada

Nicholson and they had one son.

Roy Hauton became a very good amateur photographer – he took pictures of my own Christening back in 1948 as well as taking the picture of the Sunday School winning the Whitton Shield in 1949. He was also a Sunday School teacher for many years.

Daughter Dorothy Hauton married Reg Harness, a regular chapel member in 1920 and they lived in Church Lane Saxilby. They had a daughter Greta who married and moved away, whilst their son Ron married local girl Jean Newcombe who was already a member of the Junior Church.

Jean was extremely involved in the chapel over many years, teaching in the Sunday School, singing in the choir, helping set up the Mums & Toddlers Group, running the Junior Choir, acting as Overseas Missionary secretary, running the Fairtrade stall as well as being editor of the Methodist News for a good number of years.

Younger daughter Olive Hauton married John Hardwick who was a joiner and a member of the Free chapel and they had one daughter Mary. Tragically in 1949 John had a massive heart attack whilst he was at evening service and died in the new chapel. Olive continued to live in the family bungalow in Mill Lane, playing an active role in the life of the Chapel, with Mary joining the Junior Church, but they moved away when Mary finished University and became a librarian. The bungalow they lived in has just been demolished and two new properties stand in the grounds.

Again and again, we see the way the generations of what might be referred to as 'dynastic' families kept the chapels so successful, coming through the Sunday School and then marrying other members of the chapel and their children following the same pattern.

Rev John Earl at Chapel Garden Party around 1950. Photo includes Jim Whittles, Joe Vasey, Ken Sykes, Pam Burton, Bert Hotchkin.

The Junior Church used to meet each Sunday afternoon in the choir area of the chapel, and naturally with Auntie Connie being the organist and choir-mistress, all the young people were introduced to music and singing. According to Gill Pacey, who was a member during the early years, it was a very happy group, always busy with some project or other but still finding the time to enjoy trips out, as well as holidays. Gerald Fox, another original member of the Junior Church remembers rather a wet holiday to Wales, with his mother having to deal with a bag of very wet clothes on his return. Another founder member was Bryan Parman who became Sunday School Superintendent for forty years, as well as being a dedicated and much respected member of the choir with his beautiful bass voice. As the story of Godfrey Memorial chapel unfolds, they'll be more about the Junior Church and what part they played over the years.

Some members of the Junior Church on an outing, taken about 1950/51.
L-R: Bryan Parman, Derek Revill, Leila Earl, Gerald Fox, Ann Parman, Pam Cox? and Muriel Credland.

The Rev Earl quickly recognised the lack of space for the Sunday School, which was full to bursting in their current schoolroom, with the primary children being squeezed into the vestry using long forms, as there was no room for individual chairs. In January 1949 he requested that the Trustees look to purchase land so that a new Sunday School hall could be built, but whilst they approved his suggestion, they stipulated it must have a flat roof so as not to obscure the stained-glass window at the back of the chapel. After much discussion over the following months, it was finally agreed to approach Dr MacPhail, who lived in the house now known as Saxilby House, to see if he would be willing to sell a strip of land behind the chapel, as well as a further strip some four yards wide to enable the car park to be enlarged. It wasn't until January 1952 that the land purchase was completed and Mr Picksley of Harby Chapel agreed to provide a privet boundary hedge, just as the Rev Earl was leaving the circuit.

The Sunday School at this time was very busy with 14 teachers involved each Sunday, and in 1950 both Mrs Doris Chapman and Geoff Atkinson became regular teachers, with Stan Goy playing the piano.

Doris Chapman was the grand-daughter of John James Skipworth, and had been much involved in the life of the Wesleyan Chapel and the setting up of the Guild. She had married Norman Chapman and went to live at the farm on Saxilby Moor, having two daughters, Audrey and Vera, and two sons, Robert and Brian, who all attended Sunday School – Mrs Chapman was a much loved teacher there for many years. Both Audrey and Vera are shown in the photograph taken when children from Saxilby won the Whitton Shield for the highest marks in the scripture exams. The family later moved into Diamond Villa in Saxilby.

Charles Geoffrey Atkinson (Geoff) was the son of Charlie and Annie Atkinson, who lived down Lincoln Road and had been active members of the Free Chapel, marrying there in 1922. Geoff was a natural leader, becoming a Sunday School teacher, leading the games and taking charge of the Christmas parties, as well as ensuring there was plenty of fun on outings and making sure everyone joined in the singing on the coach coming home. He was a member of the Magic Circle and could entertain people for hours with his magic skills, as well as taking charge of the Scout group in the village. It was through his involvement with the Scouting movement that he met Jean Dixon, a member of Bailgate Chapel, and asked her to come out to Saxilby once a week and set up a Cub Pack. They married in the early 1950s and set up home on the High Street and together they were leaders of the Scouts and Cubs in Saxilby for all their married life. Unfortunately Geoff suffered with ill health throughout his life and died at the age of 44 in 1970.

Jean carried on living in Bridge Place with children Janice and Ian, later marrying Derek Revill, who had a daughter, Denise, and they continued to live in Saxilby for the rest of their lives. Many people will remember Jean, as she was connected with the Cubs all her life. She had a fine singing voice being a steadfast member of the Chapel Choir as well as the Drama Group. For much of her life she worked at the Post Office in the village so was well known and much loved throughout the village.

Some of the older children of the Sunday School were willing to enter the National Scripture Examinations which took place each year, although this did involve extra preparatory lessons, which in 1949/50 were run by Rev Earl, Mrs Talks and Mrs Lang. As you'll see from the photograph below, taken outside the chapel, children from Saxilby Sunday School won the Whitton Shield that year for gaining the most marks in the county for the Scripture Exams. Quite an achievement for a village Sunday School.

Sunday School with the 'Whitton Shield' 1949/50. *From Back Left:* Rev John Earl, May Johnson, Leila Earl, Gwen Pacey, Jean Valley, Peter Hodson, Rosemary Talks, Muriel Credland, Vera Chapman, Shirley Britt, Brenda Clifton, Madeline Newton, Tony Smith, Mrs Talks, Mrs Lang, Audrey Chapman, Veronica Clifton, Mary Hardwick, Irene Britt, Frank Credland, Dawn Johnson, Gill Pacey, Roberta Talks, Anne Parman.

As there was such little space available for concerts, public teas and events of a secular nature, the Chapel regularly turned to the Village Hall, which of course, had been a previous home for many of the congregation. As part of the sale agreement, a member of the Chapel Stewards was always appointed to represent the Methodist Church on the Village Hall Committee, so there was still a close connection between the two organisations, and many events took place there during the 1940s/50s before the new Sunday School hall was finally erected in 1961.

My mother was often asked to accompany local shows that were being staged either in the Village Hall or WI Hut and on one occasion when I was in the Brownies, she played the piano when the Guides and Brownies put on the show 'Snow White and the Seven Dwarfs'. It was so successful that a neighbouring village asked for it to be repeated, but during that performance, a lighted candle carried by one of the dwarfs set fire to her cotton-wool beard. Panic broke out on the stage as well as in the room behind where the Brownies were trapped, but quick as a flash my mother helped pulled off the burning beard before anyone was injured, picked up her heavy winter coat and managed to put out the flames. Within five minutes of the commotion, calm was restored and the show continued. The only downside of the story was that my mother's new coat was ruined and she had to revert to her old one.

It was during this period that the Nativity Play, written and arranged by Hilda Clark and her daughter Marjorie Ford, started to be staged, and because there was no platform in the chapel, it took place in the Village Hall. It was a wonderful adaptation of the Christmas story, with two narrators linking the various scenes together, and with enough parts for everyone who wanted to be in the production. Mrs Clark and Mrs Ford always made sure it was an excellent production, even though all the songs/ carols (often with multiple verses) had to be learnt by heart, so it was a huge undertaking. It was extremely popular and always finished with the audience standing and singing 'O Come All Ye Faithful'. Memories flood back of being very young, yet taking part in one of the plays at the Village Hall – most of the primary Sunday School girls were angels – absolutely freezing as I was dressed in a white cotton shift, bare feet, with tinsel round my head and wings made from wire/cotton wool, waiting to go on stage to sing the carol 'Rocking' with two of us having to lay a piece of fur over the crib. Whilst the play wasn't put on every year, it was a tradition which carried on for many years, taking place in the chapel once the new platforms were available, and was always a wonderful way to show people the real meaning of Christmas.

The 'Sisterhood' was a weekly meeting held in the Sunday School room, set up in May 1940 for the lady members of the chapel to come together, commencing with a hymn and a prayer with the remainder of the hour being spent knitting or sewing together. Each member subscribed one penny each week, although this was optional. They also began organising a Bring & Buy Stall and Rummage sale followed by a public tea, which was also held in the Village Hall, all proceeds going to the war effort. Each year they would organise a special Sisterhood Sunday, with a guest preacher and music organised by my mother, Connie

Rawson, who would train the ladies to sing one or two anthems at the service. When I read through the officers of the group, we find people like Mrs D Lang, Mrs C Credland, Mrs J Mansfield, Mrs J Fox, Mrs C Oxby, Mrs M Grayson and Miss E Skipworth all taking on roles during these early years. The group continued to run every week for the next 40 years, before eventually changing their name to the *Women's Fellowship*.

By 1948 they were organising an outing each year, visiting places like Mablethorpe, Cleethorpes and the Dukeries. They put their knitting and sewing to good use by organising a Sale of Work in the summer, usually at the home of Mr & Mrs Lang down Lincoln Road, with funds being split between Church funds and their own account which went towards holding an Annual Tea in December for members, who would all take part in a light-hearted programme of music and poems.

They also started giving a Sacred Play on the evening of Good Friday, which was repeated for several years. Gill Pacey tells me that her mother was taking part in one production, but Gill had been taken into hospital to have her appendix removed and until she knew her daughter was out of surgery, she refused to take part. Of course in these days parents couldn't be with their children, in fact visiting was only three times a week!

When Mrs Lang was forced to retire through ill health, Mrs Earl was invited to become President of the Sisterhood, setting up a tradition that the Minister's wife would always be invited to be the President.

Chapter 9

1952–1957: Optimism and Growth

In 1952 King George VI died quite suddenly and the following year villagers found themselves celebrating the Coronation of Queen Elizabeth II, with her husband Philip, an ex-naval officer, impatient for change in the new world order. The few homes which had television sets were full to overflowing on Thursday 2nd June 1953, as the first live broadcast of a Coronation was beamed across the world, allowing those with access to a TV to view the 8000+ guests arriving in all their splendour to attend the ceremony in Westminster Abbey and watch the celebrations as the new Queen and her family stood on the balcony of Buckingham Palace. I'm sure many people will remember exactly what they were doing that day. It was an iconic moment, symbolising to people everywhere that the darkness of the war years was ending and a new dawn was breaking, heralding a period of regeneration and innovation. Forget the antimacassars on the chairs, the pantry with meat safe and the barometer in the hall, now there were new houses with central heating, vacuum cleaners, washing machines, and fridges, as well as the arrival of pop music.

The Rev Earl, who had had been a much-loved minister for four years, was moving on in the summer of 1952, but he was leaving behind a chapel now filled with optimism and enthusiasm due to his efforts with the young people. The Junior Church was flourishing, encouraging members to become involved in all areas of life at the chapel, and the Sunday School was once more buzzing with excitement.

Fortunately the next Minister to arrive was able to build on all that had been achieved and ensure that growth within the chapel continued. His name was Rev William F Podmore and he quickly became known by the young people as 'Uncle Bill'. He was charismatic and full of enthusiasm for his role as Methodist Minister in this rural area, an ex-RAF Padre who had experienced the war and became extremely well regarded both in the community of Saxilby and all the villages he looked after, even though some of the congregation found his intellectual sermons a little difficult to understand. His wife Muriel was somewhat different, being quiet, reserved and happy to stay in the background looking after their daughter Pamela. For many people the Podmore family quickly became dear friends and I remember many happy times on Christmas Day when, after eating a huge Christmas lunch with Albert Little and family at Ingleby Hall, they would join our family festivities, with his daughter Pam and my sister Pauline, becoming close friends.

Muriel & Bill Podmore. Photo taken during a rather damp Guild outing to Derbyshire

At this time, despite the assessment being raised to pay a bigger stipend to the Ministers, they were always extremely poorly paid, having to rely on the goodwill of members to help furnish the manse and other necessities. It was the Rev Podmore who needed help to buy a new car, as one night when he was driving home from one of the many meetings he had to attend, the steering wheel of his car literally came away in his hands! Fortunately one of the wealthy farmers attending the chapel quickly provided him with a replacement vehicle, which enabled him to continue his work around the Section.

During Rev Podmore's ministry, sadly a number of

well-known and much-loved people passed away, and in 1952 the chapel mourned the loss of Mr Dickerson 'Dick' Lang, who had been at the helm of the Free Chapel for most of his life and had been the driving force for the amalgamation with the Wesleyans in 1937. He and both his wives had hosted countless garden parties at their house down Lincoln Road over the years and had been devoted teachers in the Sunday School. The following year Percy Smalley and Mr Mayfield died, with Edith Skipworth, Tom Wilson and Joe Valley all passing away in 1956. They were all familiar and much-loved members who had played key roles in the chapel over many years and were greatly missed.

This meant that the membership needed new people to keep the chapel successful and in 1954 they were fortunate to welcome Charlie Mackinder, who came to work for Lawson's Nursery, living in the house where Oaklands now stands. His wife Edith, sons Norman and David and daughters Sylvia and June all became active members of the chapel, with Charlie being an excellent local preacher. I remember listening to him preach on many occasions and he always had the knack of bringing everyday life into his sermons and making them really meaningful. Norman became a missionary, Sylvia was active in the choir and Sunday School, with June going on to run the SPCK bookshop in Lincoln.

Although land had been purchased for extra Sunday School accommodation, there were still no funds to build anything of adequate size, so members of the congregation took advantage of the area and used them as allotments. However, the problem of overcrowding in the Sunday School continued and when the vestry was out of action for a time, meaning the primary department had to occupy the schoolroom, the junior classes had to take place in the chapel, as well as using the old Centenary Chapel across the road on occasion. That building had been rented to Rose Bros since closure, but the lease contained a clause stating that one room at the back had to be available for use if required. As a very small child I remember using this on the odd occasion for my Sunday School class, but I never liked it as it was dark and full of cobwebs.

Being a Sunday School teacher was a big commitment and the list of tutors necessary to ensure all the many classes continued to function as they should, went through many changes around this time with regulars Donald Valley and Jean Mansfield leaving the village, and new people such as Barbara Madry and Anne Revill being asked to become teachers. Mr Michael Clark had been asked but he too was moving to Sutton-on-Sea so was unable to accept the invitation to help out. Mr Bob Talks had been Acting Superintendent of the Sunday School following the resignation of Mrs Lang, who was moving away following the death of her husband, but eventually Frank Credland agreed to take on the role.

In 1953 the Sunday School Anniversary celebrations followed the familiar pattern of having two separate anniversaries with the primary/junior classes on one Sunday, followed by the seniors the following Sunday. My mother, Connie Rawson, was in charge of the music, whilst the teachers arranged poems and songs for the younger children, with a suitable demonstration service being sourced for the older ones. On the Monday following the second Anniversary, the usual parade round the village was organised with Mr Talks booking the Village Hall, requesting the loan of the harmonium from Mrs Askew and arranging the sports and games in Mr Scott's field. Rev Podmore approached certain farmers regarding the drays. The tea was organised by Mrs Frank Ford, who was in charge of refreshments for all the many events during this period.

This photo was taken in the late 1950s by which time lorries had replaced the drays and at least had side panels so were slightly safer. Not everyone can be identified but the picture includes Sylvia Mackinder, Jean Newcombe, Gwen & Gill Pacey, Muriel Credland and Connie Rawson. The lorry was provided by J Bradshaw & Sons from Sturton.

It was difficult for the children to be seen and heard performing their Anniversary poems and songs, so eventually new staging was built which fitted in place of the choir stalls. It was a mammoth task to put it in place, requiring many willing helpers to haul three huge platforms from their storage home in the coal bunker and erect them over the tiered steps after removing the choir pews, which were themselves incredibly heavy. Once the stage was in place, the rehearsals took place in earnest and the anticipation of all the children grew, as they loved being part of such a special event. New clothes were always purchased for the occasion and the chapel was full to the doors as grandparents, aunts, uncles and other family members turned out in force to hear the children perform their poems and songs. The excitement continued on the Monday for the tea and sports/games followed by climbing on the wagons and setting off around the village singing their songs as they went, with villagers turning out to wave and drop coins in the collecting boxes.

Sunday School children also had their trip to the seaside to look forward to each year, provided they had 50% attendance during the year, usually taking place early in July. Buses would be organised to go to either Skegness, Mablethorpe or Cleethorpes (usually rotating), leaving Saxilby at about 8am and returning from the coast at 7pm, so it really was a full day out – wonderful if the weather was kind, but not so good if it rained. Games of rounders or cricket would take place on the sands, with a visit to the swimming pool or paddling pool, walk on the prom with Mr Whippy ice cream and of course a fish 'n chip tea before leaving. The ride home was always enjoyable as the teachers ensured there were big bags of sweeties to hand round whilst singing songs such as 'We'll be coming round the mountain' or 'Ten green bottles', something everyone looked forward to for weeks ahead as it was always great fun.

The practice of prize giving continued to mark good attendance at Sunday School and in 1950 the primary children had a prize valuing £4 and the senior children £6, with a copy of the Methodist Tune Book given to every member of the Junior Church. Then there were Christmas parties for the youngsters – Primaries/Juniors followed by the Seniors, which included tea, with games such as 'passing the orange under your chin', musical chairs, 'sucking peas through a straw' and 'the station game'.

As well as Sunday School parties at Christmas, the members and friends of the chapel had their own celebration annually, usually held in January and in 1955 it was held in the WI Hut in William Street with a good number attending, although some people didn't like having the photograph taken, so not everyone present is on the picture.

Saxilby Chapel Party, 1955. Back Row L-R: David Mackinder, John Valley, Bryan Parman, John Edwards, Unknown, Raymond Snelling, Len Smith, John Parman, Bob Chapman, Charlie Mackinder, Herbert Valley, Bill Podmore, John Rawson, Dennis Edwards, Geoff Ford, Jean Atkinson, Gill Pacey, Pauline Friend, Gwen Pacey, Mavis Wells, Muriel Credland, Tom Ford, Jean Newcombe, Muriel Garmory, Betty Hurst, Ann Jones, Sheila Britt, Harold Newton, Mary Gelder, Dora Valley, Dorothy Newton, Miry Smith, Ivy Day, Geoff Atkinson, Connie Rawson, Margaret Boswell, Alma Hauton, Elsie Foster, Sylvia Mackinder, Betty Valley, Walter Harley, Sheila Germany, Muriel Podmore, Tom Day, Joe Vasey, Hilda Clark, Gladys Parman, Doris Harley, Edith Mackinder, Jennifer Ford, Eileen Hunt, Mary Hardwick, Madeline Newton, Anne Parman, Pat Todd, Christine Brown, Evelyn Hughes, Stephanie Clark, Marjorie Ford, Jack Hauton.

It was at the chapel parties that I learned dances like the Gay Gordons, the Barn Dance and the Military Two Step, a way of mixing and chatting with the older members who would sit round the edge of the room enjoying watching the young people dance and chase round playing games. It was the chapel family in action, strengthening the bond of all ages coming together in a happy and meaningful way.

As part of the Aldersgate Circuit, young people were encouraged to take part in various events open to all the chapels in the circuit, to promote a sense of fun and friendship. At the Sunday School Festival of 1955, held in

April over three days at Hannah Memorial and Portland Place Chapels, the programme shows a number of children from Saxilby taking part, as well as the Junior Church Choir.

It started on Tuesday evening with a Bible Quiz on the 'Stories of Joseph' with Saxilby coming third out of eight entries. On the Thursday night two recitation classes were held for girls and boys under 8 years of age, with two solo classes taking place for the 15-20 year ages. The Saturday was a packed afternoon schedule of recitation classes, solo singing and bible reading, spread over both chapels, so youngsters could be performing in Portland Place for one class, then having to cross the High Street to go to Hannah Memorial for another. Tea was served at 4.45pm whilst the Arts & Crafts section was being judged, with classes for drawing, handwriting, miniature gardens and cookery.

Saxilby children taking part were:

Under 8 years	9-10 years
Diane Ealam	Sandra Bowles
Barbara Hewis	Ann Brown
Lorna Hill	Patricia Brown
Merle Johnson	June Mackinder
June Mackinder	Pamela Hutchinson
Jennifer Rawson	Margaret Johnson
Elizabeth Smithson	Kathleen Storey
David Ford	Ivan Shaw
Philip Hodgson	
Barry Johnson	
Stewart Newton	

11-12 years	13-14 years
Evelyn Britt	Jennifer Ford
Stephanie Clark	John Parman
Pauline Rawson	
David Edwards	
Malcolm Frith	
John Smithson	

In the evening session, which was attended by the Mayor of Lincoln, the Choir Competition, Choral Speaking and the finals of the Bible Quiz took place.

The Junior Church from Saxilby entered the Choir competition with the test piece being three verses from the hymn 'Immortal Love for Ever Full' but the middle verse had to be sung to a different tune to verses one and three. Saxilby won the competition, being awarded the 'Hawkings' Shield with the adjudicator announcing that Saxilby's middle verse, was absolute perfection!

Later in the year the Circuit Sports & Field Day was held in the playing field adjacent to the Moorland Park chapel, and I remember it being another fun day out. There were various stalls and sideshows to keep all the youngsters amused, as well as excellent refreshments. No details are shown in the programme, but there were lots of us taking part in various events and I believe Saxilby did very well in the relay races, but not the tug-of-war!

There seemed to be lots going on at the Sunday School during this period and of course the children were also involved in other chapel activities like the annual Garden

Parties which were held on the August Bank Holiday Monday – which was on the first Monday of August during the 1950s.

As the Saxilby Methodist story has already told us, garden parties were a great way of raising funds as well as encouraging the wider community to come along and enjoy the afternoon and make new friends. We've already covered many such events held at Rose Villa, The Pastures and Ingleby Hall, but over the next decade, an annual event was arranged on August Bank Holiday Monday each year in Dr MacPhail's field, adjacent to the chapel, in fact there was a narrow entrance in the hedge, to allow people to come through to the chapel for the tea, which was laid out in the schoolroom, as well as to use the toilet facilities. These regular events were organised each year by a Committee, who met regularly to plan the occasion with meticulous care.

Over the next few years we see many familiar names on the Garden Party Committee. Tom Day was always secretary, with members including Bob Talks, Jim Whittles, John Rawson and various members of the Valley family. In the early years, Mrs Frank Ford used to be in charge of refreshments, but by 1955 Mrs Herbert Valley had taken over the buffet tea. Members of the Junior church were more than willing to get involved with Sylvia Mackinder, Madeline Newton, Muriel Credland and Dennis Edwards on the Committee. Rev Podmore was always the Chairman during his time as Minister and would make arrangements with Dr MacPhail for the use of his field, as well as visiting local farmers to ensure there were two pigs as prizes as well as bales of straw and hay to ensure the games like skittles could have a safety barrier.

The various stalls followed a familiar pattern being run by the different organisations within the chapel, with individual people arranging the games, usually along the lines of:

Jumble Stall
Bottle Stall
Cake Stall
Sweet Stall
Handkerchief Stall
Gift Stall
Produce Stall
Ice Cream & Drinks
White Elephant Stall
Hoopla
Bran Tub
Skee-ball
Bowling for a pig
Skittling for a pig
Coconut-shy
Scouts tree ride

For the little children there was a hobby-horse, courtesy of Mrs H Valley and a large rocking-horse courtesy of Mrs G Ford. New ideas were tried. In 1956 there was a fancy dress parade, in 1957 there was a 'hidden treasurer' game with a 10/- note buried in the sand and in 1958 rose-button holes were made and sold. The Gainsborough Salvation Army Band came one year.

Handbills and posters were produced to advertise the event, as well as an advertisement in the Lincolnshire Chronicle and Echo and of course an invitation was sent to all the chapels in the circuit. Every year there was a short service in the chapel at 2.45 where the Chairman would introduce the person who had been invited to open the event, with Dr MacPhail doing the honours in 1956. These events, whilst a tremendous amount of hard work for all involved, were very profitable, ensuring funds remained healthy, as well as being a thoroughly enjoyable afternoon and a way of welcoming the community into the life of the chapel.

The Guild continued to have a successful weekly meeting, and looking at the varied programme for the Winter Session 1995-56, no wonder it was such a popular group. The Rev Podmore was President, with an active committee, made up of young and older members ensuring the many different events were well organised. There were visits out to a Circuit Rally, a Circuit Bible Quiz and a visit to Collingham Guild and in November the Guild Players put on two one-act plays in the Village Hall with Barbara Madry producing both plays and other Guild members helping backstage. The week before Christmas was taken up with carol singing, which was always great fun, usually with a large number of young people going round the village streets singing all the familiar Christmas carols, and of course others following them with collection boxes when people came out to listen. One of the first times I ever went inside a pub in the village was with a collection box, but the customers always seemed to enjoy the festive singing and gave generously as the money raised always went to the National Children's Homes. On New Year's Eve there was a party in the schoolroom with entertainment and games organised by Geoff Atkinson and John Valley, followed by a 'Watchnight Service' in the chapel when everyone would gather to worship together and welcome in the New Year.

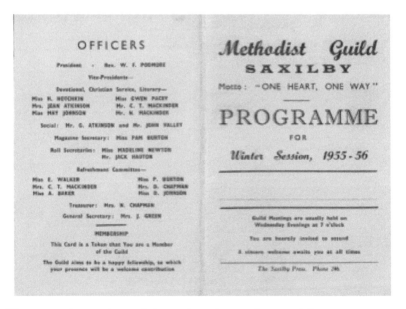

The usual rotation of devotional, service and literary events carried on, inviting various guest speakers, with the Junior Church taking one of the literary events including poetry and satirical readings, Mrs Madry showed slides of her holiday in Spain, Bailgate Young People came to speak on Christian Service and there were the Devotional meetings with different Ministers as well as local preacher Charlie Mackinder.

Guild outing about 1950 , with Rev Earl in centre front, with daughter Leila on his shoulder. Others include Geoff Atkinson (looking out window),Mrs Atkinson, Derek Revill, Gwen Pacey, Ann Parman, Pam Burton, Rosemary Talks, Ivy Green, Muriel Credland, Hilda Hotchkin, Mr & Mrs Tom Day, Norman and Donald Valley.

Throughout the years of Methodism in the village, the choir was always at the heart of services. My mother had been in charge of the music ever since the new chapel opened and it soon became recognised as an excellent centre of music and singing. 'Auntie Connie', as she was known by most people, was also the organist, and I remember occasions when I used to sit next to her during services and the steward would bring her the list of hymns for the service, probably only ten minutes before it started. At the same time as playing the organ, she'd get me to hold up the list of hymns and scan through to see if there were any the congregation wouldn't know, quickly finding alternative tunes if necessary, so that the singing always went well. It seemed as if she knew the number for every hymn!

It became a tradition for the choir to give a cantata on the evening of Good Friday, usually alternating between the Crucifixion and Olivet to Calvary, as well as putting on a special concert on the Saturday evening of the Choir Anniversary, plus special singing at events like Christmas.

The picture below was taken at the end of a very successful concert in the mid-1950s.

L-R: Joe Vasey, Harold Newton, Bryan Parman, Bill Mansfield, John Parman, Michael Clarke, Walter Harley, Mr Egerton, Ivy Day, Marjorie Mansfield, Jennifer Ford, Dora Valley, Mirry Smith, Jean Atkinson, Mary Gelder, Gill Pacey
Muriel Newton, Jean Newcombe, Ann Parman, Hilda Clark, Betty Valley, Alma Hauton, Gwen Pacey, Doris Harley, Marjorie Ford, Sylvia Mackinder, Evelyn Britt, with Connie Rawson and Rev Bill Podmore either side

It was impossible for Connie to play the organ and conduct, so for some special events she started to ask one of the choristers from the Cathedral if he would come over. His name was Charles Clarke and she had met him through the Lincoln Musical Society; he was a bundle of fun, always telling jokes and stories and making the choir laugh, but he was also an excellent organist. When he left, Mr Hatton from North Scarle came to assist, but in 1957 Eric Smith, the baker from the shop on the corner of William Street, became the official assistant organist, making life much easier. By 1959 Eric and his wife and his father, who lived with them, all became members of the chapel, with Eric being secretary of the Trustees' Meeting for many years and their children all attending Sunday School. Muriel Credland, a former member of the Junior Church, also started to play the organ in the late 1950s, becoming an assistant organist, a role she held for the rest of her life.

Throughout the years there had been several problems with damp both in the back part of the main chapel and the vestry, where dry rot was eventually identified. Apparently the field on which the Godfrey Memorial Church was built had a natural underground spring on the part where the back section of the chapel was built, causing issues with flooding in the underground coalhouse, as well as being the primary cause for the issues of dry-rot, which necessitated a huge amount of work during the early 1950s. It meant that for a few weeks Sunday services were held in St Andrew's Mission Church by kind permission of the Church Officials. When the work was finally complete, the chapel had been painted throughout, including the previously dark roof beams, using a variety of light/bright colours, which completely transformed both the Chapel, the Sunday School and the Vestry.

The inside of GM Chapel following redecoration. The original dark beams have now disappeared.

Also of concern was the heating of the building, which was quite inadequate, and members regularly complained of feeling cold, especially at morning services. When the chapel was built there was a ducted 'hot-air' system installed, which meant a large boiler had to be lit and stoked and eventually the heated air would flow in through a large grille in the chapel, which was positioned just behind the pulpit. You can imagine how uncomfortable it was for the preacher who had hot air blowing in his neck the whole time, although moving the pulpit to the opposite side did help alleviate that problem. There had been various attempts to rectify the issue, not least lighting the boiler a whole day earlier, which meant the fuel costs soared and the stoker had to be paid more, yet it didn't seem to help much. It was a matter which kept regularly appearing on the agenda at meetings, but it took until 1964 to change the heating system completely, when overhead electric heaters were finally installed and the boiler removed.

Chapter 10

1957–1962: Singing the Changes

It was all change for the chapel in the summer of 1957 as Rev Bill Podmore left the village at the same time as the new Lincoln North Circuit was formed, meaning Saxilby members had to say farewell to a much-loved Minister as well as leaving the many friends they had made from the old Aldersgate Circuit.

As the Methodist story told us earlier, the overlapping of the many chapels in Lincolnshire after the Union in 1932 had always been problematical, solved to some extent by the formation of the Aldersgate Circuit in 1944 but in the fullness of time it was apparent that further modification was necessary. After several years of difficult negotiations, a scheme dividing Lincoln Methodism into three circuits – Lincoln North, Lincoln Central and Lincoln South – was approved in September 1957. Saxilby Chapel had to say goodbye to chapels such as Hannah Memorial, Portland Place and others which moved to the Central Circuit, and get used to now coming under the umbrella of the big town chapels of Wesley and Bailgate in the North Circuit, and our section of village chapels now incorporated Sturton, Stow, Hardwick, Newton, Fenton and North & South Clifton. It was a big upheaval for all the chapels, but the wheels of change continue inevitably to turn.

At the same time as the new circuit was beginning, the new Minister Rev George Thompson moved to Saxilby with his wife Betty and three daughters, Sheila, Pauline & Heather. He was a Yorkshireman whose last ministry had been at the Hunstanton and Docking Circuit in Norfolk, having served in the army during the war, seeing service in France, Belgium and North Africa. He was different in many ways from the Rev Podmore, being quietly spoken and gentle in character, but he was resolute in his evangelical work, especially amongst young people. However, there was one rather large downside to his coming to such a rural area, which was that he couldn't drive a car and had to rely on public transport or the willingness of members to get around the section!

Rev Thompson soon made a start with the matter of the old chapel by insisting Rose Bros. formally be issued with a notice to quit. Grace Blanchard started as the new caretaker and her brother Tom Ford became the stoker/gardener and together they made the premises look really well maintained. Hilda Clark and her daughter Marjorie Ford offered to provide a 'Children's Corner' where the pulpit had been and a lovely light wood table was placed to hold the font and two small vases for flowers each Sunday, together with a beautiful picture of Jesus surrounded by children. Renewed efforts were made in trying to build a new hall for the Sunday School, which was really full, as well as the Junior Church having over 20 members. These included Venetia Boyer, Evelyn Britt, Alan Brit, Ann Brown, Christine Brown, Brian Chapman, Stephanie Clark, David Edwards, Mary Gelder, Gerald Gregory, Pamela Hutchinson, Gill Pacey, Pauline Rawson, Donny Shaw and Carol Wells.

The influx of new members into the Junior Church helped the group go out into the smaller village chapels to conduct services, play the organ or harmonium where there was no regular organist and sing either as soloists or part of a choir. Several older members were now leaving the village as Bill Mansfield, Jennifer Ford, Madeline Newton and Mary Hardwick said farewell. The *Methodist Recorder* gave some prominence to a very unusual Order of Service for Young Peoples' Day devised by members of Saxilby Junior Church.

The young people helped enormously when the Rev Thompson organised a Mission at Fenton (a small village about three miles from Saxilby) which was to be led by two young men from Cliff College, Len Ball and Malcolm Pears. Leaflets and programmes inviting the people of Fenton to come to the meetings were distributed and the

Junior Church organised the social hour for the Saturday evening, as well as playing the harmonium for all the evening meetings. The Mission was quite successful and the young musicians from Saxilby continued to help out accompanying services for some time afterwards, not always too willingly as apparently the harmonium at Fenton was not an easy instrument to play.

Another initiative to keep the older children involved in the church was 'Youth Squashes' (dances), which had begun just before Rev Thompson arrived but he was much enthused by them. They took place during the winter months, initially at the Village Hall, but later in the chapel's own School Hall, whereby there would be music, dancing, games and of course food, with an epilogue to close. It was the era of early pop music featuring Cliff Richard and Elvis Presley, and because the events were open to everyone in the Section, it was an excellent way for the young people of neighbouring chapels to socialise. Transport was provided in a variety of ways, music by way of a record player and games by Bryan Parman and helpers, with a large number of volunteers providing food and drink. I remember spending the afternoon helping prepare the buffet by making 'hedgehogs' with sausages, cheese and pineapple on cocktail sticks.

In order to maintain the membership of the chapel as older people passed away and younger people moved away, new ideas were always being trialled. One idea became known as 'People's Services' where members of the congregation would volunteer to take the service, choosing their own format, giving a reading rather than a sermon, and invite friends to come along. They became very popular and were usually held once a month, instead of the traditional evening service. Sometimes an organisation like the Sisterhood or the Guild would arrange them, other times just one or two people. It was a less formal way of introducing new people to what happened inside the chapel and showed how the members were adapting to the changing world.

Before Rev Thompson came to Saxilby he had never been particularly interested in the music of the chapel, but after being in the village for just over a year he was much impressed with the singing, sharing these thoughts with the choir: 'It's through you that I've discovered what a great contribution music makes to worship'. He then put out feelers about bringing the Sunday hymn singing programme on the radio to Saxilby, and on 3rd May 1959 the community hymn singing, known as 'Sunday Half Hour' was broadcast live from Saxilby Chapel. It was quite unusual for the programme to come from a village chapel although there was a combined choir of both Methodists and Anglicans, with my mother Connie Rawson conducting and the organ played by John Blaikie from the Church. With Saxilby being a village in agricultural Lincolnshire, it was broadcast on 'Rogation Sunday' with hymns, chosen by the BBC, built around the theme of 'Divine Renewal' illustrating God's renewing power, not only in the world of nature but also in the lives of people and nations.

It was a very exciting occasion as the radio crew arrived with all their equipment and took over the entire vestry, running various tests throughout the day in conjunction with the control room in Manchester, even changing the positions of some members of the choir, so the voices were more evenly distributed. I remember my mother being terribly nervous because despite weeks of rehearsals, the programme was going out live and anything could happen, especially as some of the hymns were completely new to the choir and every verse had to be perfect. Even the congregation (admitted by programme only) had to practise standing up without making a noise – feet firmly on the ground before attempting to stand! The programme was introduced by BBC Staff Announcer, Randolph Herley, the Rev Thompson gave a blessing at the close and the singing went brilliantly with my mother receiving numerous letters from people around the country congratulating the choir. There was only one letter of complaint, which said the singing of hymns was much too fast, but then chapels are renowned for their enthusiastic singing!

THE METHODIST CHURCH
(GODFREY MEMORIAL)

SAXILBY ———— LINCOLN

"SUNDAY HALF HOUR"

A Programme of Community Hymn Singing
to be Broadcast by the B.B.C. on ——

SUNDAY, MAY 3rd, 1959

at 8-30 p.m.

To be led by the Combined Choirs of the

Church of England & Methodist Church

Organist: •   •   •   •   JOHN M. BLAIKIE

Conductor: •   •   •   - CONSTANCE E. RAWSON

Hymns Introduced by: •   B.B.C. STAFF ANNOUNCER

Prayer and Benediction by: -   •   REV. G. THOMPSON

SOUVENIR PROGRAMME

Hymns

For the beauty of the earth

'Noricum'

O Lord of heaven and earth and sea

'Almsgiving'

The glory of the spring how sweet
'Dorking'
O Lord how happy should we be
'Innsbruck'
Lead us, Heavenly Father, lead us
'Mannheim'
Lord, her watch Thy Church is keeping
'Everton'
God is working His purpose out
'Benson'
Father, who on man dost shower
'Quem Pastores'

Following the broadcast, whenever a preacher couldn't go to one of the smaller village chapels, Gill Pacey would take her Dansette record player and play the record which had been made of the event, so the congregation could either join in with the hymn singing or just sit and listen.

When the excitement of the broadcast died down, the question of a new building for the Sunday School was finally addressed, especially as by now the chapel had started its own Brownie and Guide packs, so the necessity for more space was yet more important. Rev Thompson's two older girls were already Brownies when they moved to Saxilby and as there was no longer an organisation in the village, he asked if any of the younger members would be willing to undertake the training and start a Brownie Pack.

Gill Pacey and Mary Gelder, both being members of the Junior Church, volunteered. Gill was the Brown Owl and Mary her assistant, with Mary leading the Guides and Gill her assistant. The Guide Commissioner came out from Lincoln to help, together with Jean Atkinson also assisting (despite being used to the cubs!)

Finally in 1959 two recently built halls were identified as possibly being suitable for Saxilby's needs, in the villages of Scothern and Gunness. Visits by some of the Trustees and Sunday School teachers to both premises reported back that a hall similar to the one at Gunness would be suitable for our requirements. It was manufactured in Gunness, North Lincolnshire by Messrs Empson & Sons, with a brick-built base, and as the wooden walls were sectional, Saxilby could have an extra section making the hall longer, allowing room for a stage to be erected at one end. There would be overhead electric heaters installed as part of the package, together with a separate kitchen, store room and entrance porch for an approximate price of £1,600. The 'New Building Account' stood at £1,369 and it was felt the extra money could be raised fairly quickly, so it was decided to go ahead, but first the plans had to go to both Circuit and District level before the order could finally be placed early in 1960. There were many delays but the building was finally ready to open in May 1961, with Mrs Bert Hotchkin from Hardwick doing the official opening.

Saxilby Methodist Church

Opening of the New School Hall

SATURDAY, MAY 13th, 1961

A SERVICE OF THANKSGIVING

Will be held in the Methodist Church at 3-30 p.m.

Special Preacher: Rev. F. O. Le SUEUR, B.A. (Chairman of the District)

Service conducted by the Rev. GEORGE THOMPSON (Saxilby Minister)

Collection for New School Hall Funds   Special Singing by the Saxilby Choir

OPENING CEREMONY and Dedication Service

WILL TAKE PLACE AT APPROX. 4-30 P.M.

Opener: -   -   MRS. B. HOTCHKIN (Hardwick)

Chairman: -   MR. BRYAN PARMAN (Sunday School Superintendent)

The New Hall will be Dedicated by the Chairman of the District (Rev. F. O. Le SUEUR, B.A.)

A MEAT TEA in the Hall

Will be Served at 5 p.m.   Price 2/6 each

"BRING & BUY" AND CAKE STALLS

A GRAND CONCERT

Will be given at 7-15 p.m. by

THE LINCOLN MALE VOICE CHOIR

Chairman: Mr. W. E. BATTERSBY (of Somerton Castle)   :-:   Collection for the Trust Fund

Saxilby Press, Saxilby. Phone: 216.

The new hall was a great success, allowing the Sunday School to expand. The Brownies and Guides had space to fulfil their many activities and the frequent 'teas' could now be held in our own hall, rather than using the Village Hall. Youth Squashes, Sunday School parties, Chapel and Guild parties could all take place on chapel premises. To finally have the space to flourish gave a huge boost to the whole congregation, as well as being an additional source of income as various village groups looked to hire the hall for their events.

Finance was a constant source of concern as the Assessment each quarter kept increasing and whilst the numbers of members around the early 1960s remained fairly constant at just over 100, there was usually a small deficit from the amounts collected in the envelopes and collection plates, to that required to pay the necessary accounts. As readers will have realised, funding of the chapels has always been an ongoing concern, with special events like garden parties and concerts always having to take place to raise extra funds. However in 1961 it was decided to organise a gift day, which was a huge success, raising enough to cover certain expenses and put £100 in the bank.

The Nativity Play was still being produced regularly by Hilda Clark, her daughter Marjorie Ford and granddaughter Jennifer Ford, and went on until 1963, when Marjorie's son David Ford took the part of Joseph and I took the part of Mary. Members of the cast still remember rehearsing in the school hall on the night of 22nd November 1963 when someone arrived with the news of John F Kennedy's assignation. Everyone was silent as the dreadful news sank in, too shocked to carry on with the rehearsal, but no one wanted to leave as we all began to talk about what it would mean to the people of America and the wider world.

The full cast list for the last performance can't be found, but here is the list for the Nativity Play which was held in the chapel on 18th December 1960 in place of the evening service. As always, a huge congregation packed

CAST OF NATIVITY PLAY 1960

Readers: Jennifer Rawson/David Ford

Mary: Pauline Rawson
Joseph: John Parman

Gabriel: Ann Parman
Elizabeth: Gill Pacey

Kings: Jennifer Ford, Muriel Credland
and Jean Newcombe
Pages: Sheila Thompson, Joan Cooper
and Susan Cash

Angels: Sally Horton, Pauline Thompson,
Margaret Lang, Catherine Horton,
Susan Lang, Maureen Lang and
Heather Thompson

Innkeepers: Mary Gelder, Merle Johnson
and Jennifer Pykett

Israelites: Margaret & Heather Johnson,
Christine Lang, Ann Brown,
Shirley Temple, Joan Cooper,
Susan Cash, Vivienne Clark,
Jennifer Price, Margaret Hewis

Shepherds: Stewart Newton, Brian Lovett
Terry Ealam, Peter & Richard Horton

into the chapel that night, using the Sunday School room with the doors folded back to accommodate extra seating. The Nativity Play was staged over many years, becoming a much loved part of the Christmas celebrations for the whole village.

The Parish Church had always held a Christmas Fair in the Village Hall each December, but now the chapel had the School Hall, it was decided a similar event could be organised, but on a date earlier in the calendar in order not to clash. In October 1961 the first 'Autumn Fayre' was held and became a regular feature in the chapel year, encouraging the village community to come along, as well as being an excellent way of raising money. Like the Garden Parties of the 1950s, the Autumn Fayre had a variety of stalls selling plants, home-made cakes, bottles, 'bring & buy', handicrafts as well as a bran tub. Tea was served in the old School Room and whilst the event was hard work, it was a way for all the different areas of the church to come together to raise funds.

One of Rev Thompson's last initiatives was to reinstate the class leaders, giving responsibility for ten members to look after approximately 10-12 members each, ensuring that everyone in the church community felt cared for. The ten people chosen to serve in 1962 were Mr Joe Pacey, Mr Tom Day, Mrs Shipley, Mrs Connie Rawson, Mrs Ivy Day, Miss Bemrose, Mrs Muriel Broughton, Mr Bryan Parman, Miss Ethel Walker and Mrs Betty Thompson (to be replaced by Mrs Elsie Foster when Mrs Thompson left in August).

This chapter ends with the decision to close Lincoln's 'Big Wesley' Chapel, which had opened in 1836 and had influenced life in the City of Lincoln and beyond for over a century. The factors involved were many and varied, but it was the movement of population out of the town centre than finally meant the dwindling congregation in the city centre could no longer support such a large building. Indeed the sadness of the closing of such an iconic symbol of the Methodism movement in the city was felt in all congregations around the county but it was a wake-up call to renew efforts of enriching services and finding ways to involve the community, who were becoming more mobile and finding other activities to participate in.

Chapter 11

1962–1974: The Chapel Lights Up

Saxilby was already seeing many new properties being built both on Mill Lane and Church Road during the 1950s, but by the 1960s development on a huge scale began, when the fields in the centre of the village were sold for housing. I remember walking across the fields to catch the school bus on Mill Lane and wondering whatever was happening, as the first bungalows in what is now Willow Close were being built. Soon the green footpaths with high hedges that had criss-crossed the village for generations disappeared, being incorporated into the housing estates. But here was much-needed housing that allowed young people like myself to be able to buy a property and stay in the village. The influx of people included those who came to work in the power industry (there were three power stations close by) and the RAF personnel who wanted to live off-camp, as well as the expansion of companies in Lincoln like Ruston & Hornsby and Ruston-Bucyrus, bringing diversity and change to the village.

When the Rev Trevor Staniforth and his family arrived in 1962, membership had fallen to just under 100 for the first time, so the new inhabitants of the village were very welcome. Initially Rev Staniforth, his wife Ena and children David and Rachel lived at Homelea, on Church Road, but as the circuit felt the manse was no longer fit for purpose, it was decided to build a new property, which incorporated a separate meeting room plus cloakroom. Before too long the family were able to move to 57 Mill Lane, the new manse.

The Staniforth family

By now grocery stores like the one I'd been brought up

in had disappeared and self-service supermarkets had become the norm. Society was changing with the advent of more people owning their own houses, cars and television sets. The impact of television was massive, with most householders having their own TV sets by the 1960s. This was demonstrated when The Forsyth Saga was shown on BBC on a Sunday evening and congregations across the country started to decline as members chose to stay at home in case they weren't home in time to watch the next episode. Saxilby's answer was for the steward on duty at the chapel to have to have a quiet word with the preacher informing them that the congregation would like to leave in time to get home to watch the programme – perhaps a verse or two of the last hymn left out? Of course there were also live religious services shown on TV on a Sunday morning, as well as hymn singing in an evening, so as people got older or less mobile it was all too easy to stay at home rather than turning out to attend a service at the chapel.

Gradually the changing patterns of family life meant that traditions within the chapel had to alter and adapt. Although the Sunday School still had over 100 young people on roll, it was decided not to have an outing to the coast by bus as most families had their own cars, and instead visit Somerton Castle at Bassingham for a picnic and games, which could be done using members' own vehicles. Before long the afternoon Sunday School was moved to the morning, with all the children spending the first part of the service in church before leaving to go to the school hall for their classes. The service on Christmas Day was brought forward to 9.30 am so that families could be home in good time for lunch and the 'watch-night' service on New Year's Eve disappeared. There was also a welcome change in the heating system of the chapel when new overhead electric heaters were installed, with wall-mounted electric heaters in the Sunday School.

With the Sunday School still flourishing, it was decided to try the idea of having a 'Family Service', whereby the junior children would stay in church with their family enjoying a service targeted at the younger generation. These services were successful in increasing the general congregation, but the number of members kept declining as regulars like John Will Valley, Albert Little, Cyril Hipkin and Joe Mansfield passed away. This meant the membership didn't get back to over 100 until 1966 when the chapel at Hardwick finally closed its doors and the members were all transferred to Saxilby. Rev Staniforth tried various initiatives to increase the congregation, including a mission similar to the one which had taken place at Fenton, but unfortunately there was little interest in the membership classes he put on. In 1965 a newsletter was produced by Mr Mobbs called 'The Messenger', which was printed monthly and distributed by a team of 16 volunteers giving full details of everything that was taking place in the chapel, as well as particulars for the services over the next four weeks. The cost of the newsletter was over £20 per annum, so members agreed to host either a coffee morning or evening event to defray the cost, as it was proving to be a popular way for people to keep in touch with what was happening at the chapel.

As the newly built properties became occupied there were new people starting to come to chapel, one of whom was Derek Davison, who was full of enthusiasm and happy to become engaged in the life of the church. He worked for the National Children's Home and in 1964 volunteered to start a Junior Christian Endeavour group which became a regular mid-week meeting during the winter months, with around 20 young people attending. Eventually he took over the finances of the church, a job he held for many years.

Young people like Theo & Jack Boothroyd, Averil & Bryan Parman and Jean & Jack Howes also moved into the village with their families. This helped the chapel remain outward looking and the happy place to worship it always had been, as they joined the choir and became involved in the Sunday School. Jean's parents, Cyril and Evelyn Marriott, also moved to the village and were committed members throughout their years of retirement – Evelyn joined the choir and Cyril took on many roles, being chairman of the property committee for a time. Her brother Graham and family also moved into the village, with his wife Glenys becoming a Sunday School teacher and daughters Rachel and Catherine involved in youth work.

One last initiative tried by Rev Staniforth before he left for pastures new was to hold a retreat weekend at the chapel entitled 'Living Church' which held small discussion groups in different areas of the chapel, coming up with new ideas for making the church more open to the large number of new people moving into the village. Whilst it wasn't a huge success, certain ideas were trialled, like having cards printed welcoming people to the village with service times and contact details for the many groups taking place at the chapel, but of course these needed to be delivered in person, a task which Jean Howes volunteered to undertake. Another suggestion was to have a rota of members standing just inside the door to hand out hymn books and personally welcome people to the service. This proved to be very successful and was an idea that was continued until the chapel closed in 2020.

Another different style of service tried was called a 'Guest Service', whereby members were encouraged to bring a guest with them. The service was made as simple as possible so that visitors should feel relaxed and not have to worry about following what was happening. For a time these services worked well, but as visitors declined it was decided to replace them with community hymn singing services, always popular with the congregation.

Sunday School anniversaries continued on two separate Sundays with the primaries going first, followed by the juniors/seniors on the second Sunday. By now there were a number of older children who formed a group called the 'Youth Fellowship' who held BBQs and did sponsored walks. The JMA (Junior Mission for All) began collecting money to help young people both overseas and at home, with two members from Saxilby – Angela Wells and Janette Holgate – being awarded medals for their collections, presented at the Circuit JMA Party at Bailgate Chapel in 1967.

At the beginning of September 1968, the Rev Keith Handscomb, wife Pam and children Stephen and Susan moved into the manse and very quickly set to work. Keith had trained as a BT engineer before becoming a Methodist Minister and whether it was because he'd been in a working environment before training for the ministry I don't know, but he quickly became a 'minister of the people', both at the chapel and in the village. He soon became known as 'Keith' and seemed at home wherever he went, with Stephen and Susan settling into Sunday School as well as making friends in the village through the primary school. Pam involved herself in the Young Wives Group and within a few months set up a 'Mum's & Toddler's Group' which met weekly in the large hall, another initiative which brought people into the life of the chapel and continued until it closed. Pam was also a volunteer in the Family Planning Service and when the family moved to Saxilby she continued her work in Lincoln, which left her no free time to automatically become the president of the Sisterhood. This caused some dissatisfaction with the older ladies, who were unaware of the changing environment of the 1960s and the implications the new freedoms were having on the younger generation.

Meanwhile at his first Council Meeting, Keith hit the ground running, so to speak. He asked to be kept informed about anyone in the village who became ill and would make time to visit. He wanted ideas for setting up 'house meetings' whereby small groups could meet regularly and also stressed his desire to work more closely with the Parish Church and hold united services regularly. Up until now the Family Services had been held on a rather ad hoc basis, but he wanted them set for the first Sunday each month, so that families would always know when they were, with the first service in December designated as a 'Toy Service' for children to bring gifts which would be received by a different charity each year. He also shared his ideas for making the Carol Service into a 'Candlelight Carol Service' as he was willing to build wooden structures to hang from the roof of the chapel, holding hundreds of candles. The chapel has always been most fortunate to have a huge tree donated every Christmas by Marjorie and Jack Wells from Broadholme, (whose three daughters, Judy, Angela & Elizabeth attended the Sunday School) carrying on a tradition which the Wells family had started many years earlier and has been much admired each and every Christmas.

The preparation for lighting the whole chapel by candles was a huge undertaking, initially taking hours of work in 1968 to design and construct the wooden batons and drilling holes for the candles to sit in. Each year these structures then had to be strung from the roof in the chapel before placing each candle, with silver foil base, firmly into each hole as well as moving the pews so there was plenty of space for people to move about, just in case of fire.

You can see how beautiful the tree looked, decorated with so many beautiful baubles and lights and reminding the congregation of how the birth of baby Jesus brought light to the world. Bryan & Averil Parman decorated the tree over many years and it always looked magnificent.

Fifteen minutes before the service took place, an army of volunteers would set about lighting the candles before all the lights were turned off and the service commenced. With the tall Christmas tree bedecked with coloured lights and the white glow of the candles, the chapel looked wonderful. So that the service could proceed unannounced everyone was handed a printed sheet which told the Christmas story using lessons and carols, plus items by the Sunday School and choir, with the Minister reading the final lesson and giving the benediction. At the bottom of the service sheet was an invitation for people to come to a half-hour Family Service on Christmas Day at 9.30 and asking the children to bring one of their presents to show everyone. What a success it was! The chapel was so full that the folding doors to the School Room had to be opened to seat the overfill congregation and the Christmas Day service was popular too, especially as the candles were lit once more. I seem to remember the youngsters taking delight in blowing out all the candles after both services!

This became a much-loved event at the chapel over many years, with people arriving up to three-quarters of an hour early to ensure they could get a seat in the main chapel. During the five years Keith was the minister he established a tradition that Christmas at the chapel was a time of celebration for everyone and an introduction to the wider community to enjoy the fellowship found within the Chapel. As the service on Christmas Day was designed to last just thirty minutes, it meant there was time for the whole family to come together, with the children happy to bring a present to show the congregation and hear the Christmas story using picture books. It was a format which worked really well as the chapel would be full, but this also had a knock-on effect because the number of people attending the Family Services increased as well.

The New Year party of the chapel became known as

the Church Social and with the influx of young parents the hall was packed with all ages enjoying the excellent supper as well as games and dancing which Bryan, Geoff and Derek provided. The sense of being part of a church that was outward looking and vibrant encouraged yet more new families in the village to come to chapel. Rachel & David Stow (known as Rae and Dave) and family moved on to Mill Lane with Dave eventually becoming a local preacher and Rae becoming a stalwart organiser in numerous different areas, overseeing all the teas and suppers as well becoming involved in the Young Wives group. Ruth & Edward Larkins and daughters came to live on Sturton Road, with Ruth becoming involved in the choir and Sunday School, as well as playing the organ. Norma & John Bean and daughters moved to a shop on the High Street and Norma soon became a teacher in the Sunday School along with Kathleen Hill, who lived on Sturton Road, and Glenys Marriott from Highfield Road.

By ensuring the Family Services were always the first Sunday of each month, Keith would try to be scheduled at Saxilby that morning so that he could take the service, making sure that the worship was truly family orientated. There was never a formal sermon, more a series of talks on a theme, interspersed with events which involved the children and sometimes their parents as well. On one occasion I remember running down the main aisle while having to toss a pancake at least four times! Whilst some older members took a deep intake of breath to witness such an activity, the younger element in the congregation appreciated the sense of being able to relate to a thoughtful message about Lent whilst their children were happy and content to listen to the stories they could understand. It was a format which was much enjoyed by everyone and when they began to serve coffee afterwards, there was yet more opportunity for people to discover the life and happenings in the chapel.

The People's Services were planned each quarter and continued to be an inclusive way of bringing the worship to the congregation in a different way. Each group of the church took turns in organising the services, from the Sunday School, Youth Fellowship, Guild, Choir, Brownies & Guides, Young Wives and Sisterhood, as well as some members who got together to lead the worship. Services combining all the chapels looked after by the resident minister in Saxilby, known as 'Sectional Services' were recommenced each year incorporating Stow, Sturton, Newton, Ingham, South Clifton and Saxilby.

Liaison with the Parish Church was put on a more formal basis with three members from the chapel being designated to work with church members to find ways and means to work together. This brought about having a United Service each quarter, two in the Parish Church and two in the chapel, with Remembrance Sunday following the usual pattern of being in the church one year and the chapel the next. This initiative led to a much closer relationship between the Methodists and the Anglicans for many years, as national negotiations continued to find a lasting pathway towards healing the separation. Over the years there has been regular co-operation with the Christian lunches taking place regularly, organised and hosted between the two churches.

As the Youth Squashes which had been held each winter continued to fulfil a need, it was felt there should be a regular meeting for the young people connected to the chapel, and in the early 1970s a Youth Club was started, meeting each Saturday evening, with various members of the chapel being involved over the years, including Ian Wallis, Jean Harness, Ian Johnstone, Neil Besley, Gwen Otter and Ruth & Graham Hodges, endeavouring to keep young people connected with the chapel.

It was during this time that the sale of the old Wesley Centenary Chapel finally took place, having taken up many hours of negotiation and letters between the tenants, Rose Brothers, and the chapel officials. The building had had no repairs for years and was looking very run down and neglected, but despite finding someone to buy the property, a clause was put in by the chapel officials that it must be demolished within six months of purchase, as they didn't want it to continue to look so neglected. This caused some issues with the sale, as Mr Turner, the local builder who was keen to purchase the building, was so busy building new houses he didn't have the capacity to demolish the building as stipulated. However in 1969 the sale was finally agreed and the old chapel was demolished.

In the early 1970s the Chapel Treasurer, Derek Davison, reported that the Assessment all chapels had to pay was to be increased significantly and as the chapel was already relying on fund-raising to pay the Assessment, there needed to be serious discussions about finances. As we know, the Assessment is based on the number of members, so it was deemed that members should be encouraged to give more, with an emphasis on joining the envelope scheme. By doing this, members would commit to giving a sum each week, regardless of whether they attend services or not, thereby ensuring the chapel would have regular money coming in to help pay the Assessment. It was also decided to put the Financial Statement for the Church on the notice board at the back so everyone could see the full picture. Coffee evenings had become a popular way of raising money, so regular events were planned as a means of raising the extra funds required with people like Judy and Geoff Brown and Sheila and Gordon Hill happy hosting events. It was also decided to have a Gift Day, whereby anyone could give an ad hoc amount to help the church.

The suggestion of holding a Flower Festival was discussed as these were proving popular at other churches, so it was decided to try one in Saxilby using the hymn 'All Things Bright and Beautiful', with each group taking one verse as their theme. The chapel would be decorated on the Friday evening and then open to the public all day on the Saturday and Sunday, with light refreshments being available as well as organ music being played by a rota of musicians, including Muriel Broughton, Ruth Larkins and Theo Boothroyd, who had started to play the organ when Eric Smith left the chapel to become full-time organist at the Parish Church. This was the first of several such events which were well supported, bringing in many people who had never been inside the chapel, as well as raising funds. The next one was held just as the Rev Keith Handscomb was leaving Saxilby in 1974, using the theme of parables with seven groups each taking a separate parable. By now I'm sure you'll have seen, throughout the story of Methodism, the pattern of the chapels always in need of funds but raising money in ways that were enjoyable and entertaining, as well as welcoming to the wider community.

One of the many displays from a Flower Festival held during the 1970s

The newer members of the chapel whose children were now attending Sunday School were playing their part in encouraging other families to come to services. Janette Woolaston, who moved into Church Road in 1973 with husband Roger and children Kim and Matthew, explained how the day after they moved in, Rae Stow was in touch welcoming her to the village and inviting her to an event. They quickly became close friends, especially as they discovered various members of each family shared birthdays. Janette had been brought up in a Methodist family and was used to helping out in all the many ways, from arranging flowers to preparing bread for Sacrament, so she soon felt at home helping out in the chapel. Ruth Larkins played a similar part in inviting Kathleen Hill and Andrea Drury to become involved in the chapel and of course as soon as you have a group of young friends together, they are happy to organise events and take part in services.

The picture on the next page of the ladies having a sponsored 'knitting day' and thoroughly enjoying themselves as they raised money for chapel funds.

Changes of governance within the Methodist Church were taking place and in 1974 the Leaders' Meetings were replaced by a body known as the 'Church Council'. Its very first meeting was held on 12 July 1974 with Rev Keith Handscomb presiding, but at the same time having to say his farewells to the officials he'd worked with over the last five years. There was also a Sectional Service at Saxilby with the chapel full to capacity as members from all the churches he'd overseen came to say goodbye to an extremely popular and much-loved Minister.

L-R back row: Gladys Parman, Jean Revill, Theo Boothroyd, Andrea Drury.
L-R front row: Jean Harness, Kathleen Hill, Ruth Larkins, Averil Parman.

Chapter 12

1974–1985: A Generational Shift

When the chapel welcomed the Rev Rodney Warden, his wife Chris and children Andrew, Matthew, Daniel and Sam in September 1974, the village centre was almost full with new bungalows and houses and the population had virtually doubled to over 2750. Brenda's Hair Stylist on Bridge Street was now offering OAPs at reduced rates on Mondays and Tuesdays, the Spar Grocers, run by Mr & Mrs Chapman at the corner of William Street, were now selling French cheese and sausages, and Jim Murphy was advertising home-killed meat at his butcher's shop at 49 High Street. The school needed to expand with 'temporary' extra classrooms and the village changed quite rapidly from being the place where everyone knew each other to appearing full of new faces. Having said that, with

Saxilby being the friendly place it had always been, the community soon came together through various groups as well as through the Church and Chapel. The United Services between Church and Chapel had been running for several years, leading to a close working relationship which continued under the ministry of Rev. Rodney Warden.

The Warden family, `Rodney' and `Chris' as they became known, had very young children but soon fitted in with Sunday School and the Mum's & Toddlers group. Indeed most things carried on as before, with the Guild, Sisterhood, Choir and Junior Christian Endeavour all continuing to benefit as the new homes both in Saxilby and the surrounding area became occupied. The People's Services were now being held each month as membership increased, welcoming people like Edith & Ron Metcalfe and Sheila & Gordon Hill as well as Rosemary Fieldson and her son transferring their membership to Saxilby. All became active members, enabling the chapel to continue feeling enthusiastic and welcoming.

When Rodney presided over his first Church Council meeting the following people were on the committee: Jack Hauton, Walter Harley, Hilda Hotchkin, Jean Atkinson, Derek & Kath Davison, Mary Connell, Jean Harness, Connie & John Rawson, Dora & Herbert Valley and Mrs Nicholson, Marjorie Wells and Cyril Marriott, all loyal, familiar people. However, as the speed of change in all areas of society was accelerating, new initiatives were needed to keep the chapel in tune with the younger generation. In 1976 Wendy

& Ben Climer moved into Sykes Lane, with children Simon, Jane & Naomi, who were in their teens and loved music, so Wendy started a Junior Choir which proved very popular. Before long a club called the 'Whotsits' began, following on from the choir practice each week, which attracted young people from both inside and outside the chapel, and for several years the group met regularly, putting on concerts at the Village Hall, raising money for local clubs.

The Senior Choir, whilst continuing to lead services each Sunday with outstanding singing, welcomed additional members from the new people who were moving into the village. The many concerts they gave throughout the year to raise funds continued to be much appreciated, with the musical performance on the evening of Good Friday, now including people from the Parish Church, still attracting a large congregation. Invitations kept coming in for the choir to give concerts across the area and to add variety to such events, they started singing both traditional anthems and part-songs but also spirituals, gospel and folk songs as well as the odd popular piece of music, interspersed with narrative poems to add contrast to the programme.

For over twenty years Saxilby Choir, under the direction of my mother, Connie Rawson, sang at chapels and halls across the county, often joined after 1976 by the Junior Choir. At the Queen's Silver Jubilee in 1977 the United Choir of both church and chapel performed at the special event to mark the event at the Village Hall. The following Saturday, 11th June, there was a Jubilee Concert in the chapel incorporating the Senior Choir, the Junior Choir and an Instrumental Group, with patriotic items including The Lincolnshire Poacher, O Peaceful England, Who are the Yeomen, The Farmer's Boy, and Non Nobis Domine, closing with the National Anthem!

The Junior Choir began staging a variety of performances including a concert in the chapel, Gilbert & Sullivan's 'HMS Pinafore', 'Joseph & His Amazing Technicolour Dreamcoat' with fantastic costumes and of course the Elvis figure and in 1981 presenting 'The Wizard of Oz' as shown in the photograph below.

The cast of the Saxilby Junior Choir production of The Wizard of Oz. Jane Broughton, Linda Harness, Julie Broughton, Kathryn Parman, Jane Harness, Sarah Stow, Tina White, Joanne Fields, Rachel Fallis, Deborah Fallis, Janet Boothroyd, Karen Page, Phillipa Quarrie, Sally Trueman, Emma Taylor, Melanie Forbes-Ritte, Ian Trueman, Andrew Forbes-Ritte, Darren Stow

The Candlelight Service was still extremely popular and every year different people within the chapel were invited to read one of the lessons. On one occasion Rodney asked Kathleen Hill, who was the Sunday School Treasurer, if she would be willing to take part, but she turned him down, explaining she would be far too nervous, only for her son Graham, who was in the room at the time, to announce that he'd be happy to give a reading! And indeed he did, so well it appears that Mrs Hilda James, one of the chapel's older ladies and quite hard of hearing, congratulated him afterwards saying 'he was the best reader by far, she could hear every word'. Graham went on to perform in the London Pride Extravaganza staged in the chapel in 1985! Kathleen was born on 25th December, so the Christmas morning service always included the congregation singing 'Happy Birthday', accompanied by the organ.

As you'll be aware by now, getting people to help in the Sunday School had been an ongoing problem over many years, although Bryan Parman was a faithful and devoted Superintendent for nearly forty years and there were very few occasions when he wasn't there, although he did have the reputation of often being 'rather last minute'! Teachers needed training and their lessons had to be prepared, so it meant dedication and commitment each week, but the young people kept coming so obviously the teachers were doing a good job and the children enjoyed themselves.

Sunday School Float for Saxilby Gala Procession 1980. The theme for that year was Noah's Ark, which is why you can see various animal masks and costumes.

In the mid-1970s Mrs Doris Chapman was still in charge of the Primary section alongside Norma Bean, Rae Stow and Theo Boothroyd, whilst Bryan was assisted in the Junior/Senior sections by Elsie Foster, Jean Harness, Kathleen Hill, Ruth Larkins and Glenys Marriott, but extra help was always needed. Wendy Climer volunteered to help, as well as Diana Kirk, who joined the Primary team, being a great help with the music as she brought along her guitar. The chapel was lucky to have teenagers like Julie Boothroyd, Denise Revill and Jane Climer willing to help as older members retired, but finding and retaining teachers was an ongoing struggle.

Another regular commitment in the Sunday School was collecting for the National Children's Home, something which had been going on for decades. The first home was founded in 1869 by a Methodist Minister named Thomas

Bowman Stephenson to provide care and shelter for homeless children in London, later adopted at the Methodist Conference and called the National Children's Home (NCH) with chapels encouraged to raise money to help support the Homes. The Guild in Saxilby always supported this, initially doing carol singing and then holding a carol concert every year to raise money. In the 1950s-60s-70s a regular form of fundraising for NCH within the Sunday Schools was called 'Sunny Smiles', which were booklets containing pictures of children who were being looked after at one of the homes and in exchange for a photograph, family and friends would be asked to make a donation for the charity. There was then an annual event in Lincoln called a 'Festival of Queens' to celebrate the money collected in the Lincoln, with each Sunday School choosing someone to be their queen. Whilst this was considered an accepted way of raising money at the time, by the late 1970s/80s it was discontinued when it was decided that the homes would be phased out and instead offer support to enable children to stay with their families. The name changed in 1994 to 'NCH: Action for Children' to better reflect the work it did and in 2008 became just 'Action for Children' (AfC). Today it is a national charity in partnership with the Methodist Church which helps and supports over 600,00 children, young people and their families in the UK every year.

By now the Brownie Pack started by Gill Pacey back in 1969 no longer met at the chapel, but as there were children attending Sunday School who wanted to join,

Janette Woolaston agreed to start the 3rd Saxilby Brownie Pack in the School Hall, helped by Jenny Forbes-Ritte (who'd originally trained as a Guide) and Mary Smith, with Steph Parman helping out in the later years. It was very successful and when Janette finally gave up ten years later, Sue Gray took it over for many more years.

Regrettably, early in 1978 the chapel was informed that the Rev Rodney Warden would be transferred in the summer, a full year before he was due to finish. The Church Council wrote letters expressing dissatisfaction to the Secretary of Conference, the Chairman of the District as well as the Circuit Superintendent but without success and sadly at the end of August Saxilby was left with no resident Minister. The Rev Michael Hughes from Lincoln stepped in to oversee the chapel and the manse was occupied by Student Pastor Mark Powell from Cliff College who came to help out for a year by taking services and attending events but the Rev Hughes had to attend all the formal meetings as well as taking Sacrament services. Not an ideal situation but it was deemed the chapel could cope for a year, and indeed they did, with the younger generation excited by having someone young and energetic at the chapel.

Wendy, Theo, Jean and Dave continued working to ensure the Junior Choir, the Whotsits Group and the Youth Club provided stimulating activities. Pastor Mark was someone who understood the needs of younger people and worked alongside Wendy to help foster new initiatives as well as a closer relationship with the adult members. He introduced a weekly discussion group which met during the afternoons at the home of Rae Stow. This brought young mums together, hosting a variety of speakers including the probation service and the NSPCC. The Sunday School teachers re-energized their lessons by using designated material and introduced more activities, as well as putting on a Nativity Play each year, with updated words and music, giving the young people chance to perform. It was during this year that Wendy's elder daughter Jane and Mark became really close friends eventually getting married! However, whilst the young people were thriving, the General Church Meeting in April 1979 were raising real concerns that attendances were declining, even at Family Services, and were looking forward to the arrival of the next resident minister.

The Rev Percy Allen and his wife Betty moved into the manse in September 1979 during a year of upheaval in the country. Public service strikes at the beginning of the year had brought chaos, with high unemployment and inflation causing real hardship to families, leading to a General Election which saw the Conservative Party sweep to power and appoint the country's first female Prime Minister, Margaret Thatcher, the daughter of a Methodist lay preacher from Grantham.

The finances of the chapel rather mirrored the general feeling of gloom in the country with another increased Assessment, showing the weekly collections would need to rise by £9 per week to even break even on last year's figures.

Quite a challenging situation for any new minister, but the Rev Allen was more mature than any of his predecessors with years of experience behind him and with a calm resolve, set about restoring the current financial crisis in ways that brought the membership together. Coffee evenings were recommenced, a book stall set up at the back of the chapel, a concert by the Salvation Army arranged and a Harvest Supper on the Monday evening after the traditional Harvest weekend. Evening services during the winter months were moved to the small hall, which would save money on electricity and lastly the charges for letting out the School Hall would need to be increased.

A cleaning rota was now in place to save on the costs of hiring a cleaner with Rae & Dave Stow organising a team of eight teams. Hopefully all these efforts would help alleviate the immediate cash crisis and more regulated forms of income could be put in place.

Cleaning Teams	Door Stewards
Janette Woolaston & Jenny Forbes Ritte	Gordon Hill
Sheila Hill & Mary Connell	Derek Davison
Betty Allen & Elsie Foster	Dave Stow
John & Connie Rawson + Gladys Parman	Mary Connell
Jean Harness & Wendy Climer	John Rawson
Kathleen Hill & Andrea Drury	Hilda James
Rae Stow & Glenys Marriott	Marjorie Wells
Ruth Larkins & Theo Boothroyd	Cyril Marriott

Gradually the efforts and cost-saving measures paid off and everyone felt much encouraged. Ruth Larkins organised the young people from the Sunday School to do a sponsored walk which raised £50 and Patrick Forbes-Ritte joined the team of Stewards, with his wife Jenny helping out at the new Brownie Pack run by Janette Woolaston. The ladies group known as the Sisterhood for the past forty years was renamed the 'Women's Fellowship', eventually becoming just the 'Afternoon Fellowship' in the later years to include both women and men. The chapel's 40th Anniversary in 1980 was a joyous occasion, the membership was back to 120 and the congregation celebrated the past and looked forward to the future. The Rev John Earl returned as special guest speaker for the weekend and a turkey dinner was held on the Saturday evening organised by Mrs Sheila Hill.

In 1982 Lincoln Methodists hosted an 'Impact Weekend' when 1200 young Methodists from all over the country converged at Lincoln, with Saxilby hosting two Youth Clubs, one from Bolton in Lancashire and the other from Workington in Cumbria. Seven of the young people from Workington spent the week before on a sponsored walk covering 180 miles as they walked all the way to Saxilby, raising money for Penrith Methodist Home for the Aged. Many members and friends helped with looking after nearly 40 young people at Saxilby that weekend, cooking, washing up and cleaning, all organised by Wendy Climer, Rae Stow and Rosemary Fieldson.

The Parish Church was now printing and distributing a

monthly magazine giving details of what was happening both at the church and in the village, called 'Foss Focus' and in 1983 the chapel was asked if they would like their newsletter incorporated into the magazine, giving it a much wider distribution. Initially it was agreed to trial this, but very quickly it became permanent and at the beginning of 1985 Neil Besley agreed to take over the job of editing the chapel news from Jean Harness.

New events and new members ensured the chapel continued to be active and exciting. Rosemary Fieldson began hosting a Tuesday 'Circle' Group, Wendy Climer led a Bible Study group each week and Norma Bean took on the task of heading up a Fund Raising Group, to co-ordinate the many different activities to keep the chapel financially secure as well as organising various activities for the young people. The chapel welcomed Jean & Ian Johnstone with their children Derek and Linda and foster daughter Becky, who was profoundly deaf, with Jean helping in the Sunday School and Ian in the Youth Club. Jean & Eric Ball also moved into the village, both already committed members with Eric being a lay preacher. They began a Bible Fellowship group at their home in Elm Close, as well as a group called 'Youth Rendezvous', which met every Sunday evening.

By the time Rev Allen had been in post for his full five year term, the life of the chapel was on firmer foundations once more as this busy calendar for 1985 shows, listing all the services and events that took place during just one year, demonstrating the commitment and devotion of all the people who volunteered in many different ways to ensure faith and fellowship continued at the chapel:

- Donations for replacing the chairs in the small hall were ongoing, with empty Smarties tubes being filled with 20p pieces.

- Evening Services were held in the small hall lead by Rev Allen and team of our own local preachers on the theme 'Living in the Covenant'.

- The New Year party held on 12th January was a great success.

- £70 was raised for the Ethiopia Famine Relief by holding a 'cup-a-soup`' lunch in January

- The Chapel Anniversary weekend and Gift day took place on 23rd/24th March with the Rev Bill Podmore travelling from Derby to take the services.

- The Sunday School Anniversary was held on 31st March on the theme of 'Sing Hosanna' with the Primary Department performing at the morning service and the Juniors in the evening using drama and music to enact the story of Palm Sunday, with tea and games on the Monday after school.

- The Choir performed the Crucifixion on Good Friday.

- On Easter Saturday there was a special coffee morning and cake stall.

- On Easter Day an 8.30 service of communion took place, followed by a Family Service at 10.30 and an Evening Service at 6.00pm with Rev Allen taking all the services.

- Coffee morning in April to hear about plans for 'Mission England'.

- Services of Baptism for Alison Linton, Gary Otter, Adam Turner, Craig Lang and Amy Rose.

- Confirmation Service for Betty & Ian Wallis who became new members at the chapel.

- Women's Fellowship Anniversary with Miss Rands and Mrs Wakelin from Lincoln

- 'Family Spring Cleaning Day' organised to give the premises a deep-clean.

- A Summer Fayre was held on 8th June with all the usual stalls, games, refreshments plus fancy dress and painting competitions. Unfortunately it was a wet day, so everything had to be held indoors but was a happy and successful event raising £320 for chapel funds.

- 22nd-29th June Billy Graham's 'Mission England' rally at Bramhall Lane, Sheffield with coaches organized from Saxilby for various events.

- August Family Service to say farewell to Rev Percy Allen.

- Sunday School outing to Mablethorpe on 28th August organised by Norma Bean.

- The Tel-a-Viv Rock Gospel Concert was held on 31st August in the School Hall to celebrate Young People's weekend, with special Youth Service on the Sunday evening, followed by the first 'Sunday Youth Rendezvous' meeting at 7.30pm.

- Weekly rehearsals begin for the concert on the theme of 'London' which was to be staged at the beginning of November.

- Circuit welcome on 4th September at Saxilby for the Rev Ronald & Mrs Todd led by the Chairman of the District.

- On Sunday 15th September there was a United Service at the Parish Church when the Rev Todd was invited to give the sermon.

- The first weekend of October was Harvest Festival, with the chapel being decorated on the Saturday afternoon in the traditional way, with the Rev Todd leading the Family Service and evening service on the Sunday. On the Monday evening there was a service of thanksgiving followed by a Harvest Supper with entertainment by the Kirk Family Singers and the sale of produce.

- The Guild celebrated their Anniversary Sunday on 20th October with a parade service of the Cubs, Scouts, Brownies & Guides, taken by Mr Cammack from Ingham.

- The Young People presented their song and dance Extravaganza 'London Pride' on Friday & Saturday 1st/2nd November in the School Hall, with thanks to Norma Bean, Theo Boothroyd and Wendy Climer. A sum of £113 was raised for the Youth Rendezvous Group.

CAST OF THE 'LONDON PRIDE EXTRAVAGANZA' 1985
Those identified include' Matt Shepherd, Melanie Forbes-Ritte, Graham Hill,
Caroline Bean, Kim Woolaston, Jane Harness, Sarah Stow, Janet Boothroyd,
Lizzie Clark, Emma & Ellie Bean, Linda Harness, Derek & Linda Johnstone,
Caroline & Helen Bean, Sarah Butler plus the Pearly King & Queen: Denis Joice
and Marjorie Wallis.

- Anne Larder and Wendy Climer were welcomed as teachers in the Sunday School, with additional help from the young people Jane, Linda, Kim, Cathie and Catherine.

- A sponsored knit took place on 18th November in aid of Overseas Missions, when a blanket made up of 5' squares was completed to be sent to Ethiopia. For those who couldn't knit, there was a simultaneous sponsored sing.

- A United Service of Remembrance was held at the chapel on Sunday 20th November.

- The Chapel's Christmas Fayre took place, raising £420 for chapel funds.

- The Festival of Queens was celebrated at Central Methodist Church on Friday 29th November in honour of funds raised for the NCH, with entertainment of 'Magic, Mirth & Mystery' plus the Lincoln & District Scout Band.

- The Sunday Youth Rendezvous meetings continued each week at 7.30pm, hosted by Eric Ball

- Gift Day on Sunday 1st December was for 'Cherry Tree House' on Skellingthorpe Road run by Carol & Stewart Newton, who would be at the service to receive the gifts. Stewart was a member of Saxilby Sunday School and Choir before leaving the village, taking part in the Nativity Play of 1960.

- The annual Carol Service was organised by the Guild for the NCH.

- Christmas Coffee Morning with cake stall on Saturday 14th December.

- Candlelight Carol Service on Sunday 22nd December taken by Rev Todd.

- Christmas Day service at 10am lead by Rev Todd.

- Coffee morning at the manse on New Year's Day.

From this incredibly long and varied list you'll notice, alongside the many familiar services and anniversaries, there is a Sunday School drama production, Gospel Rock concert, outings to the huge mission rally at Sheffield, the beginning of Youth Rendezvous Group as well as the song and dance Extravaganza London Pride, all activities striving to keep the next generation involved in the life of the church during this period of social change. Yet even with all these efforts, records show there was a continued decline in the number of young people coming to Junior Church and other events, as the coming generations challenged the familiar routines established by their parents and grandparents.

Chapter 13

1985–2000: The Challenges of Change

Young people weren't the only section of society challenging traditional routines of the past. It was also a time of turmoil within the country's industrial heartlands as large manufacturing companies, which had been the life-blood of the economy, contracted and closed. The miners' strike which had caused bitterness and hardship for twelve long months, as workers tried in vain to stem the tide of closures, came to an end, leaving communities devastated. Yet at the same time the future heralded new innovations as mobile phones arrived, the first heart-lung transplant took place and Tim Berners-Lee came up with the idea of the World Wide Web. Workers finally drilled through rock separating the UK and France and TV cameras filmed them walking between the two countries for the first time since the Ice Age and before long the Channel Tunnel became operational.

Meanwhile the Rev Ronald & Mrs Dorothy Todd arrived at the manse in September 1985 coming from industrial Lancashire, a very different area from rural Lincolnshire. In the Heywood district where they had come from, there had once been 40 active mills, now reduced to three, giving him first-hand experience of the hardship caused by closures. Yet because Ron's father's family were all from Lincolnshire, he wasn't unfamiliar with the rural settings of his wider pastoral care which included chapels like Sturton, Stow, Newton, Ingham and South Clifton. The many events which were already on the calendar at the chapel ensured he soon became a familiar face and friend to everyone as he attended everything he could. He had a quiet, gentle manner, was an excellent listener and always made people feel that he cared, which endeared him to everyone, young and old alike. Like his predecessor, Rev Todd came to Saxilby for his final ministry as he would be retiring in 1991, but he soon settled in and obviously enjoyed his years in Saxilby so much that he and Dorothy decided to stay on in their retirement. After visiting Dorothy and Ron in Saxilby, their long standing friends Sylvia and Jack Gibbons decided to join them in their retirement, and the chapel was delighted to welcome them as they quickly became much loved active members.

To acknowledge the generational shift, a new hymn book was launched, with some of the old familiar hymns disappearing, whilst others had words and tunes modernised, something that was not to everyone's liking but a necessary step to try to keep relevant in the wider society. Also introduced at the same time was a Mission Praise book, which incorporated choruses and songs by modern composers that could run alongside the Hymns & Psalms book. It was suggested that the chapel should have one of its own preachers planned once a month, when the congregation could sing some of these newer hymns and songs. Jean Ball also suggested that a Worship Consultation Group be set up made up with representatives from all the different organisations to consider how things could be improved in a coordinated way.

The Sunday School arranged for a 'Walk of Witness' with friends from the Anglican Church, starting at 10.30 in the chapel for a 'tableaux', after which there would be a procession uphill to the Church, where the cross which had been carried would be planted. This became an annual ecumenical event, changing in format as the number of young people declined, and began starting at St Andrew's Centre on the Memorial Ground, processing to the High Street with a stop for prayers outside the village sign, stopping again at the chapel for a hymn, readings and prayer, before going to the church, where the cross was planted by the main door. Everyone then enjoyed a welcome cup of coffee and hot-cross-bun in the Church Hall. In later years, the Chapel introduced the idea of a Flowering Cross, a wooden cross wrapped in wire, which was planted in the front garden of the Chapel on Good Friday. At the end of the service on Easter Sunday, members of the congregation were invited to take flowers from the window ledges, then go outside and decorate the cross. For the rest of the week the bright yellow daffodils made the cross stand out as a beacon of light and hope to the village.

A Holiday Club was introduced at the end of August which ran for a week, led by Norma Bean with help from various members, and in 1987 there were 60 children attending. Sunday School outings to the seaside had been reintroduced and that year there were three bus loads of young people and friends who spent a rather showery day in Mablethorpe! The Holiday Club ran for a number of years and the Sunday School saw a small increase in members, but not in the large numbers hoped for, although the Youth Club was doing well with between 25-30 young people each Saturday evening, with Mrs Gwen Otter now helping out.

In 1988 the chapel welcomed Ruth and Graham Hodges, who had recently got married and set up their first home in Saxilby, having met through the MAYC (Methodist Association of Youth Clubs). Ruth was doing teacher training at Bishop Grosseteste College and Graham came to work for European Gas Turbines in Lincoln. Ruth's parents had been missionaries in India before coming back to the UK, where her father became a Methodist Minister, so she had been brought up within the family life of a chapel. Before long she became a willing volunteer, helping Norma run the Holiday Club as well as taking over as Cradle Roll Secretary, a post she held for many years. She ensured families who came to have their children baptised in the chapel had a link person to keep them informed about the different activities which were available for their children through the years. In 1989 the Sunday School Anniversary in June put on songs and drama at the morning service, followed by a faith lunch with over 70 people taking part, yet the plea for more helpers in the Sunday School continued to be a regular constant theme.

Both Ruth and Graham were musical and together with new members Jackie and Mike Cove and their children they set up a band, which worked well in the early 1990s. Graham and Mike both played the guitar and Steven Cove played the drums, with Ruth joining some of the young people to lead the singing. As part of the District Youth Orchestra and Choir, they took part in a big festival at Skegness, which everyone thoroughly enjoyed.

The suggestion from the Worship Consultation Group of a 'Songs of Praise Service' was well received, especially as the chapel was fortunate in having such talented organists, musicians and singers. Members were asked to choose a favourite hymn and to explain why they had chosen it, giving everyone the opportunity to share their stories. Reflecting back on the many wonderful hymns enjoyed over the years, these services were very popular and uplifting. However, there were several occasions when people felt overcome with emotion when singing particular hymns, usually for personal reasons, so efforts were made to avoid certain ones, not an altogether satisfactory outcome for other members who happened to enjoy them. The Senior Steward told me the most favourite hymn by far was 'Great is thy Faithfulness'.

In the year 1990 it was the chapel's 50th Anniversary when both Rev Keith Handscomb and Rev Bill Podmore returned to take special services. My parents, Connie and John Rawson, celebrated their Golden Wedding anniversary that weekend and after the morning service on the Sunday, the whole congregation gathered for coffee and cake (made by my father, who was renowned for his splendid fruit cakes). Just prior to the anniversary the Chapel had also had students from Cliff College run a mission in the village with the theme 'Growth within the Church' which led to Jan Himsworth, Diane Maltby and Andrew Court start coming to chapel, with Alan Measures joining thanks to his friendship with Jack Gibbons. The Youth Fellowship now met every Sunday evening in the small hall and a new 'First Steps' group for mums and toddlers began meeting weekly. During that year Dorothy and Ron Todd organised a holiday to visit the Oberammergau Passion Play in Bavaria and many people from Saxilby joined other Christian groups to witness this famous spectacle which has run every ten years (with exceptions due to war etc) when the people of Oberammergau re-enact 'The History of the Passion and Death of Jesus Christ'. The Passion Play started in 1634 when the Black Death wiped out whole populations in the Alpine valley of Bavaria, and is now a tremendous tourist attraction.

The following year, in August 1991, Rev Todd's ministry at Saxilby came to an end, but as they had already made plans to stay on in the village, Ron had to absent himself from duties at Saxilby for a year, in order to give the new incumbent time to settle in. Dorothy continued to worship at the chapel taking over the choir and playing the organ with Ron returning to Saxilby after his time away.

Dorothy & Ron had organised many Christian holidays in the past and their expertise in arranging such holidays during their years at Saxilby enabled many members of the chapel to travel to places 'within a family group' they would never have visited on their own. Photo of Dorothy, Ron and life-time member Gill Pacey on one of their many holidays

During their years at Saxilby they organised two trips to The Holy Land, two trips to Oberammergau, and holidays to Madeira, Switzerland, Austria, Slovenia, Croatia and Italy. Following Ron's ill-health, they started taking holidays in the UK, taking 'block bookings' on Eagre coach holidays, which is why, for those readers who still enjoy Eagre/Wilfreda Beehive trips, there is a collection/drop-off point at Saxilby

Chapel, thanks to Dorothy's negotiating skills. Following Ron's death in 2005, Dorothy continued to organise trips, often taking small groups for short-breaks in London to see the shows, but also started arranging overseas trips again, going back to Oberammergau in 2010 as well as holidays on the Rhine.

Gill Pacey, a life-long member of Saxilby chapel, went on every single holiday and has wonderful memories of them all, telling me how much travel has broadened her mind and given her opportunities she could never have imagined.

Norma Bean with the Nigerian guests.

During this period the chapel welcomed four guests from Nigeria who were visiting the UK as part of a Circuit sponsored initiative. Whilst in the village, they were invited to a morning service at the Parish Church where the Rev

Edward Cook asked them to speak to the congregation, which they did, but finished by spontaneously singing 'Amazing Grace' with no accompaniment but in wonderful harmony. It was totally inspiring and when they finished there was complete silence before the congregation burst into rapturous applause.

In September 1991, the Rev Lesley Whitehead moved into the manse, becoming Saxilby's first female minister. Lesley was supported by her husband Jerry and children Jamie & Katie. Jerry was also an experienced local preacher, and he quickly became the Local Preacher Tutor for the circuit. He trained both Margaret Mason and Jan Himsworth to become local preachers based at Saxilby during afternoon sessions, which suited them all, as they could work around collecting the children from school.

Lesley hadn't been in Saxilby long when my mother was taken into hospital, and whilst not knowing her well, she showed great devotion in caring for her throughout her illness, often visiting late at night after services or meetings. In fact she visited her on the night she died, just two days before Christmas. It can't have been easy for Lesley as a relative newcomer to take her funeral at the end of December as there we so many people who wanted to take part. The chapel was packed with family and friends from across the country who came to say farewell to someone who had given her life to Methodism. A wooden screen was built by Ron Metcalfe in memory of 'Auntie Connie' which provided a draught-shield from the open door, as well as giving children an area they could go to play. There was also an engraved plaque to celebrate her many years as organist and choir mistress.

The Henry Jackson Organ at Godfrey Memorial Chapel 2020. Originally installed in the Free Chapel in the 1880s, it was played by Connie Rawson, my mother, for over 70 years.

One of Lesley's first priorities was to look at family worship and develop this in conjunction with the Sunday School, which as always was struggling to find teachers. Avril Kemp had recently left the village, Margaret Mason had resigned due to concentrating on training as a local preacher and after seven years as leader of the Primary section, Catherine Bean moved away to start work. Caroline Bean, Catherine's sister took over in the Primary section, assisted by Rosemary Fieldson, but it was a difficult time, although the Sunday School still took part in the Gift Day in December that year for 'People First', the local charity which supports children in India, with Nick Hansen the co-ordinator attending in person to receive the sum of £210 which had been collected. They also visited the local care homes, singing carols for the residents. Eventually the Sunday School was renamed the Junior Church and over the coming years Helen Fieldsend, Jan Himsworth, Ruth Hodges and Andrew Court worked to look after the younger members of the chapel.

The Junior Mission for All (JMA) had been run over several years by Norma, Catherine and Caroline Bean but was taken over by Ruth Hodges in 1992, and Ruth continued to organise the collection boxes which children took home to raise money supporting the Methodist Church's World Mission fund and Mission in Britain Fund. Each year there was a special service when all the children involved were given badges/certificates, dependent on the number of years they had taken part. In 1992, badges were given out to ten young people: Caroline & Helen Bean, Rachel & Jessica Besley, Victoria Mellis, Kate & Jenni Waite, Helen Mason, Melanie Plaskett and Gary Otter. Certificates were presented to the members who were now moving on: Linda Harness, Avril Kemp, Derek Johnstone and Catherine Bean.

The Treasurer, Ron Metcalf, informed the Church Council that although the chapel was in a relatively good position, in order to meet the Assessment fund-raising was still essential and members should be encouraged to give more in order to be able to help those in need in this country and across the world. Regrettably Ron died quite suddenly in 1994, but thankfully Graham Hodges stepped in and took over the finances for the next four years, putting all the figures 'on the computer' which made life easier for future Treasurers. It appears the message of more generous giving was heeded because the collections increased, as well as the number of fund-raising events with a supper dance, gift day, jumble sales, songs of fellowship, autumn fayre and garden party at Hazel and Ken Simons. Raffles which had always been forbidden as a way of raising funds, were finally allowed on church premises, although not initially welcomed by some, but gradually became another means of income. Mrs Lillian Allison, whose sons had all attended Sunday School, left a sizeable bequest and the hall lettings increased with the Slimming Club and Aerobics Club meeting regularly, meaning the finances were in a position to embark on some much needed repairs and renewals.

The chapel benefited from a new and much more efficient gas central heating system, making services warmer and more comfortable, which together with new double-glazed windows, also saved on energy costs. It was also decided to refurbish the small schoolroom and after a ballot of members, rename it 'The Wesley Room' with the evening services in 1995/96 being held there during the winter on the theme 'Health & Healing' with five speakers taking a different aspect each week, culminating in 'Death and Bereavement'. Lesley was interested in healing both body and mind and encouraged Wendy Climer, who was a trained counsellor, to start the Bereavement Support Group, which met every other Tuesday morning. A number of members helped Wendy over the years including Pat Hydes, Sylvia Gibbons, Violet Priestly, Ann Williams and myself, enabling the group to run for many years, offering sanctuary to people whether they attended church or not, young and old, men and women. It was a way of showing the church in action within the wider community as people from the surrounding villages were welcomed too. Each year a special 'Bereavement Service' would be held, where people could come and light a candle to remember their loved ones.

The chapel started to use fairly-traded coffee for all their coffee mornings and before long Jerry Whitehead organised a Traidcraft stall after Family Services. This organisation was a Christian initiative set up to change people's lives through trade by buying goods from sources in developing countries, which gave workers a better deal, enabling them to have a better quality of life, and for people here to shop knowing they'd played a part in creating a fairer and more caring world. When Lesley and Jerry left in 2006, Jean Harness took on the responsibility of Traidcraft within the chapel, and it became a Fairtrade Church in 2002. She continued in the role until leaving the village shortly before the chapel closed.

Dorothy Todd had taken over the choir from Auntie

Connie and in June 1995 organised a Family Service by presenting a musical 'Saints Alive' featuring the choir and young people, which told the story of Pentecost. The Youth Club still met each Saturday evening, there was a Junior Church Anniversary followed by a family lunch and as part of a circuit day entitled 'Celebrating Children' Saxilby took the opportunity of hosting professional actor Bill Varnam, who led a group of 25 children aged 5-11 through song, dance and drama to explore what it means to be part of the world today. Music continued to flourish under Dorothy's leadership with a programme of sacred music on Good Friday performed by a united choir of chapel and church members, as well as a musical in December entitled *Carol of Christmas*. Meanwhile Jonathan Nowell, son of Rev Terry Nowell, started a choir known as the Circuit Singers and performed at Lincoln Baptist Church followed by *Gospel in the Waterside* in Lincoln, which was repeated in Saxilby as well as singing in Bailgate Chapel during the Christmas Market.

Rev Tania Fowler arrived in the summer of 1996 with her husband Colin and daughters Emma and Rebecca. Tania had been a radiographer before she trained for the ministry and came to Saxilby as a probationary minister. Emma and Rebecca became members of the Junior Church as well as the JMA along with Donna and Julia Maltby, while Colin turned his hand to posting. As it was Tania's first ministry she was supported in her work by local preacher Jan Himsworth and she quickly settled into the cycle of events at the chapel. The idea of a 'Tots 'R' Us' at the community centre was trialled and the Family Service became known as 'All Age Worship' yet despite being well liked and successful in her work, life was challenging for Tania and after much careful consideration and counsel from her mentor, she decided to resign and leave Saxilby in 1998.

Tania's sudden departure left Saxilby and all the villages in the section without a Minister, but Saxilby was fortunate to have Margaret and David Watkinson, who had recently retired to the village after many years in the Methodist Ministry and were willing to help out. So with the help of the Circuit Leadership team and Saxilby stewards, life for the 80 members in the chapel continued without too much disruption but obviously there needed to be a replacement Minister.

In the summer of 1998 the Rev Nigel Hannah and his wife Eileen arrived at the manse to step into the vacancy. Nigel was different from any of his predecessors, being more reserved and traditional in style, but someone deeply committed to social justice, with his letters in the Methodist section of the Foss Focus magazine focusing on issues of poverty and inequality. He was also an excellent pastoral leader, visiting anyone suffering from stress or ill-health, as well as becoming renowned throughout the village for the support he provided to those going through bereavement.

Nigel & Eileen Hannah

It was never easy to arrive at a section which had been used to arranging its own affairs for some time, but with good grace on all sides, Nigel soon settled in and during his five years in Saxilby life at the chapel continued to run relatively smoothly. One of the first events on the calendar that September was an 'Alpha Course' which was a completely new venture for the chapel. Churches everywhere had been aware that congregations across all religions had been declining but in the 1980s a young curate named Nicky Gumbel took over the running of the Alpha Course at the Holy Trinity Church in Brompton, known as HTB, and made it appeal to many of the young professionals in the city who, although often earning large amounts of money, recognised there was something lacking in their lives. Alpha involved a series of weekly sessions exploring the Christian faith, with each talk looking at a different question around faith, designed to create conversation, beginning with a meal and during the ten week course included a day or weekend away. The course became a huge success and quickly spread to other religions and countries around the world. Sir David Frost, whose father was a Methodist Minister and who was himself a local preacher, presented a series on ITV about the Alpha Course, giving it yet more publicity. There would often be over 500 people attending one of the courses run by HTB in London, with hot meals provided so participants could go straight from work, which would require an awful lot of organisation.

At Saxilby 22 people enrolled and whilst some were already members of the church, there were others who were interested to learn about or renew their faith. Regrettably the chapel's Alpha didn't mirror the success it was having elsewhere but by running it, showed that every effort was being explored to encourage new members.

The JMA was still doing really well thanks to Ruth Hodges, and at the All Age Worship in November 1998 the Rev Hannah presented almost twenty badges/certificates to Molly Hodges, Megan Broxholme, Joe Graves, Emma and Rebecca Fowler, Julia and Donna Maltby, Natalie and Katherine Bond, Christine and Helen Runnalls, Sarah and

Rachel Howells, Michelle Hall, Jessica Besley, Victoria Melless, Helen, Caroline and Catherine Bean.

Regrettably Dorothy Todd resigned her leadership of the choir owing to Ron's poor health and for the first time the chapel was without a choir to lead the services. Fortunately Wendy Climer had already formed an ensemble known as the 'Saxilby Seven' to sing the new songs from Mission Praise when it first came out, so could step in to lead the services, indeed it eventually became known as The Worship Group and would go out to other chapels and take services. As the name suggests, initially there were seven members in the group, but over the years, much to the amusement of some, the numbers could vary from five to nine or ten, but during their time included Wendy Climer, Dorothy Todd, Jean Harness, Theo Boothroyd, Muriel Credland, Jean Johnstone, Joan Head, Violet Priestly, Jean Revill, Gill Pacey and myself, with Stan Goy accompanying on the piano.

Stan had recently returned to the village with his wife Eva, having spent his early years in Saxilby attending the Wesleyan Sunday School before becoming a teacher, as well as learning to play the organ. He often said 'it felt as if he had come home'.

Another link to the past disappeared when the pipe organ, built over 100 years ago, began suffering from the effects of the cold, damp atmosphere in the building during the week (the heating operating only being on for Sundays), so instead of spending money on a complete overhaul it was decided to purchase an electric organ/piano. A Music Fund Raising Group was set up and various events took place, including a summer fair, cheese & wine evening, quiz, concert by the Foss Folk Choir and of course several coffee mornings.

Seven singers from Saxilby outside the Cathedral, taking part in the Wesley Celebrations in 1989. Members on that occasion were Jean Revill, Joan Head, Wendy Climer, Theo Boothroyd, Jean Johnstone, Bryan Parman and Dorothy Todd.

Meanwhile life at the Chapel continued with regular meetings of the Guild, Women's Fellowship, Bible Study Groups, Prayer Meeting and the Bereavement Support Group. Christmas services were still popular with the Gift Day funds going to STRUT (a local charity) and the 'Cakes & Carol' event and the Candlelight Service both having good attendances. Door stewards in 1999 were a mixture of older and newer members, including Nancy Angus, Harry Brown, Helen Fieldson, Elsie Foster, Jack Gibbons, Jean

Johnstone, Janet Kemp, Dorothy Newton, Gwen Otter, Gill Pacey, Hazel Simon and Doreen Walker.

As many readers will know, Christian Aid is a global organisation helping poverty and suffering throughout the world and during the 1950s an initiative was started called 'Christian Aid Week' to raise extra funds through doing a door-to-door collection. In Saxilby this involved a joint programme between the Parish Church and the Methodist Church to deliver and collect envelopes to every house in the village, which ran for decades and took a terrific amount of organisation. People from the chapel took approximately half the village, organised over the years by people including Bryan Parman, Jack Gibbons and Ruth Hodges who would ask volunteers to cover sections and knock on doors, not always an easy task but very worthwhile. In 1998 the Church and Chapel raised £1000 each, meaning the village of Saxilby sent £2000 to Christian Aid.

This wonderful achievement, together with money raised through various collection boxes over the year for Missions within the Methodist Church, gave members a renewed sense of hope and encouragement as the country prepared for the new Millennium.

Chapter 14

2000 – 2021: Looking to the Future

Worldwide celebrations marked the start of the new millennium with fireworks, parties and relief that the 'millennium bug' predicted to cause a global computer meltdown didn't materialise! Locally 'The Millennium Clock' was installed on the outside of the Village Hall and Saxilby Chapel held its own 'New Year Hot Pot Supper' party followed by a quiz and games for all the family. Lincoln celebrated with a new musical, 'Hopes & Dreams' by Rob Frost, which was performed at The Lawn with an all-age cast of singers, dancers, actors and musicians drawn from local churches and chapels in the area, while the Cathedral hosted a special service called 'Christians Unite' bringing hope for the new decade.

It was a period of yet more growth in the village, with

two large housing projects applying for building permission – one at the top of the village in Church Lane and one at the bottom, behind Mill Lane and Lincoln Road. Despite being refused locally, both developments went to appeal and won! Everyone in the village had expected that it would be one or the other, but not both, and once more there was a dramatic increase in the population which took a while to come to terms with. At this time Saxilby still had Tim Corner delivering milk to people's doorsteps and two fish & chip shops, and volunteers were always needed at Strut, the local charity shop on Bridge Street, although the Post Office decided the time was right to upgrade their office and take on foreign currency and passport work, along with expanding the sorting facilities to facilitate the growing number of postal staff required to service the new houses.

The year 2000 was also the 60th anniversary of Saxilby Chapel and plans were drawn up for a Gift Day and coffee morning, incorporating a 'Thanksgiving Tree' and an exhibition of memorabilia and photographs, all of which were very successful. Rev Trevor Staniforth was invited back to take the services on the Sunday, using the theme of 'Praise and Thanksgiving', which was much enjoyed, especially the hymns chosen, which were sung with enthusiasm by the congregation. One idea to mark the 60th Anniversary which was talked about but didn't come to fruition was to write a book about the history of the chapel, but hopefully some twenty years later that is being rectified!

The August Holiday Club was still taking place at the

chapel and as a follow-up to that, Ruth Hodges started a monthly group called 'Club-Up' with help from Jan Himsworth. It was an opportunity for children aged 8-12 to continue to meet together, even if they didn't attend chapel on a regular basis, incorporating singing, games, crafts and discussions. It was yet another way of encouraging parents to come along and see what the young people were involved in, as the group took part in services. New members were welcomed as Phyliss & Gordon Daws and Sue & Simon Kent moved to the village and quickly became involved in the chapel.

Whilst not directly connected to the Methodist Church, the Saxilby Youth Band had started rehearsing in the chapel on a Thursday evening, open to all young people between the ages of 8 and 18, whether they could play an instrument or not, as tuition was available. In order to help the band get established the chapel helped out by only charging a very small sum for the hire of the room, with the band playing at various events there over the years.

For a while the chapel felt buoyed up by the celebrations and some new members, but the steady decline in numbers continued, with just under 70 members on roll, meaning the membership had nearly halved in the past 20 years, although I'm sure no one would have envisaged the chapel closing within the next twenty years. Many familiar faces had passed away in the last ten years and the next generation, which for so many years had provided continuity in the chapel's congregation, was no longer around. For more and more people, Sundays were becoming the day to do the family's supermarket shop or enjoy the many sporting events taking place. What could be done within the village to try and attract people who were feeling disillusioned with religion? Whilst Nigel was well regarded by many for his care and compassion in the community, others were coming to the opinion that a change of direction was needed to encourage growth, taking the decision to request someone younger and more charismatic to take over.

The Rev Duncan MacBean, his wife Laura and children Liam, Shaun and Euan arrived in 2003, marking a new chapter for both the chapel and the Lincoln North Circuit, as the family had 'upped sticks', moving to Saxilby from South Africa. Born in Durban, Duncan had worked in management with Spoornet (the equivalent of British Rail) before he entered the ministry after he experienced an life-changing moment, 'being filled with an incredible peace and heard God calling him', and became a lay pastor for two years. During that time he started to think about coming to England to see the home of his grandfather, who had served at Dunkirk, and he eventually decided to take the plunge and emigrate. His wife Laura has always been a committed Christian and worked alongside him wherever his work had taken him, so it felt as if Saxilby chapel was getting two ministers, not just one. Indeed Laura went on to train to be Deacon.

Duncan & Laura MacBean

The chapel welcomed this young and energetic couple with open arms, although some of the congregation were surprised to see their new minister arrive on a motorbike and dressed in black leather! With their boys swelling the numbers in the Junior Church, they set about initiatives to bring in young people – out came the choir stalls, which had stood empty for a number of years, and in came a music group, incorporating Simon Kent on the cello and Graham Hodges on the guitar, along with various singers. Messy Church was started once a month in the school hall, when children and their parents were encouraged to come and worship in a totally new way, with activities for the children, whilst their parents could drink coffee and chat with members or listen to Duncan talk about how being a Christian could change their lives. There was also a regular Saturday afternoon film show where families enjoyed being entertained, complete with sales of ice cream in the interval.

Sue and Peter Walker arrived in the village around the same time and as Peter was quite a whizz on the computer, he set about building a website and bringing in new signage, thus enabling the chapel to come up-to-date with technology. Videos which had been made of some of the services could now be accessed via the website, giving people a taste of what was happening at the chapel as well as advertising events like the Harvest Supper, which included games for the children and entertainment for all, organised by Peter Walker, Gill Pacey and Jean Harness.

The Junior Church was still running on a Sunday morning, although not always great in numbers, and various new initiatives were started:

- A Young Mums' Bible Group at the manse on a Wednesday morning, as well as a Youth Group on a Friday afternoon.

- 'Messy Church' became known as 'Café Church' where the Junior Church would be selling cakes and lollipops to support Action Aid as well as taking an active part in the All-Age Worship which continued each month.

- The kitchen in the school hall was refurbished in memory of Rosemary Fieldson, who had been a devoted and much loved member, naming it 'Rosemary's Kitchen'. It was skilfully done by Arthur Hydes, Ron Harness and Ben Climer, enabling bigger and better functions to be catered for. (When the hall was later demolished, the kitchen was transferred to the vestry, along with the name plate for the door.)

- Duncan started an Emmaus course, designed to welcome new people into the Christian faith, as well as trialling an 'Alpha Male' course at the manse.

- The Circuit in Lincoln was also doing its part in encouraging younger people into the Christian faith with a bus kitted out to become a travelling youth centre wherever it stopped, called the 'GodPod' – for a time it called at Saxilby each week, when church members including Sue and Peter Walker, Jean Johnstone, Alan Measures and others would be on hand to talk to young people in a safe and warm environment.

- Theo Boothroyd and friends used to visit two of the retirement homes in the village and conduct a short service, playing for them to sing along, which was much appreciated.

Unfortunately these initiatives did not prove to be as successful as had been hoped, and after just two years Duncan had to scale back his involvement in the village to take on responsibility for the chapel at Ermine, as declining membership across the county meant there were fewer ministers available and he had to go where the need was greatest.

Saxilby had managed before when Rev Tania Fowler had left suddenly, so again we saw the Circuit Leadership team assist the stewards and senior members to form a team to ensure the smooth running of the Chapel for the next three years, but we were very pleased when the

Rev Jo Lightowler and her husband Andrew moved to the manse in the summer of 2008. Jo was a probationer, so the extra support of the team eased her into the challenges of looking after Saxilby as well as the villages of Newton, Ingham and Sturton, and assisted her vision of involving the community more.

Renaming the building to appear more 'user-friendly' was an idea trialled, with the main church becoming 'the Sanctuary', the vestry 'the Quiet Room', and 'the Wesley Room' continuing to host the regular coffee mornings and other events. Café Church was moved to four o'clock, as was the Candlelight Carol Service, trying to encourage people who no longer wanted to turn out for six o'clock services. A new group called 'Soul Spa' was started on a Wednesday afternoon led by Jane Jones, as an overspill for the increasing numbers at the Midweek Fellowship

Jo and Andrew arrived at Saxilby with no family, but within the first two years the congregation was delighted to hear they were expecting their first baby and by the end of 2010, Jo had not only become mum to baby Thomas, but was now ordained as a Methodist Minister, with baby Matthew arriving before the family left Saxilby, Fortunately the Circuit helped out once more by arranging for Margaret Mason and Alan Measures, two of our own local preachers, to take on many of the services, including the Café Church. It was a demanding time for them both, as they were working during the week and then having to be available to take Sunday services. Alan also became the Senior Steward, liaising with the Circuit to ensure the smooth running of the chapel continued.

Unfortunately the finances of the chapel suffered a blow when the School Hall was declared unfit for purpose, having been built 50+ years previously with virtually no foundations, and had to be demolished. This meant the letting fees dried up almost overnight, resulting in a serious loss of income, although efforts were made to use the Wesley Room where possible. The regular coffee mornings continued but now coffee was served in the main chapel, thanks to the flexibility of the individual chairs which had replaced the long rows of wooden pews allowing comfortable small-group settings.

The inside of the chapel, showing the individual chairs which had replaced the rows of seating.

The chapel at Stow had closed several years earlier, but now we see the village of Newton-on-Trent ending its long association with Methodism, as the small but devoted congregation felt it was no longer feasible to keep the chapel running, a pattern which was happening across the country as more and more of the smaller chapels dotted across the countryside were closing their doors for the last time.

Just before Jo and her family left, there was an exciting event in the village when the Olympic Torch procession came to Saxilby, being routed along the High Street. The chapel took the opportunity to set out chairs all along their frontage and serve tea and toast from a marquee in the car park. To be part of such a special event as the torch, which had passed from hand to hand over thousands of miles, was now being carried through the streets of Saxilby to cheers and applause, was a truly memorable occasion.

There was now a growing recognition that individual churches like Saxilby which had a predominantly older congregation would benefit from a co-ordinated 'Circuit Youth Fellowship'. This meant young people from the village could travel to Lincoln to take part in youth events where they would meet like-minded people of their own age, but it was with great sadness that the chapel had to finally acknowledge youth work at Saxilby, which had been such a bedrock of the chapel over 200 years, had come to an end. The demolition of the School Hall also saw the Toddlers' Group, which had been started as a chapel initiative nearly 50 years ago and had been running non-stop, having to relocate to the Village Hall.

Fortunately, although the Toddlers' Group had become

independent of the chapel through the years, when they moved to the Village Hall, Sue Walker organised a group of volunteers from the chapel to support them by going along to do the refreshments each week. This went on right until the Covid lockdown in 2020, enabling the mums and their children to engage with 'the chapel ladies' and retain a valuable link within the community. Jean Harness was one of the volunteers, meaning she'd come full circle, from being a founder member of the group back in 1970 to helping out some fifty years later.

Following Jo's departure Saxilby found itself without a resident Minister once more, but the Circuit stepped in to help and for two years members were fortunate to be looked after by the Rev Andy Burrows from Lincoln, who was very popular with the congregation. Jean Johnstone was the Senior Steward at the time and together with the other stewards, who were now responsible for the day-to-day activities, the chapel continued to provide faith and fellowship within the village. The evening service was discontinued but all the other regular meetings took place, with the Saxilby Youth Band filling the chapel with music on their Thursday evening rehearsal, the Walk of Witness on Good Friday, Harvest Festival and the Carol Service all reaching out to the community.

Rev Helen Hooley moved to the manse in 2014 with her husband David and teenage children Jessica and Daniel. Helen had completed her degree in Theology and Ministry at Durham University before she arrived in Saxilby, and with her background experience, was someone with the ability to deal with change. David had been appointed to the staff at Lincoln College and both children settled into secondary school in Lincoln, although whether they'd ever had the experience of living in a village, I'm not sure.

Before becoming a Methodist Minister, Helen had worked in engineering and capital project management before becoming a Fellow of IET with particular interest in graduate training and development, encouraging young people, including women, to consider a career in engineering through leading engineering activities in schools.

Saxilby Section had always included responsibility for a number of other nearby villages, but as these chapels closed over time, Helen's role was expanded to oversee other churches in the area, as well as Saxilby, and she eventually found herself responsible for the pastoral care of Scothern, Welton, Burton Road and St Giles in Lincoln, so she was constantly under pressure to 'manage the decline' as numbers across most churches continued to dwindle. The two circuits in the Lincoln area combined becoming known as the Lincoln Methodist Circuit, with just six Ministers and one Superintendent to cover the whole area, a far cry from the 1950s/60s.

Helen's ministry in Saxilby included 'Section Services', which enabled all her churches to come together on a rota basis, meeting in different churches each month, as well as encouraging people to attend evening services in Lincoln at either Bailgate or Burton Road.

Regular monthly coffee mornings were held in the Wesley Room to raise money for chapel funds on occasions, alongside charities such as Christian Aid, Mercy Ships, Air Ambulance and Traidcraft, which proved very popular and became a regular meeting place for the community to come together.

A Lent Study programme consisting of four sessions was rolled out across the section, meeting in Saxilby on two occasions each week, leading to the Good Friday 'Walk of Witness' and Easter Services.

Jonathan Nowell, the local singer and songwriter, who had directed the Circuit Choir, came to Saxilby to give a Live Concert in aid of the Ebola Victims and the Lincolnshire Air Ambulance as part of an initiative of building a kinder more caring society in the face of rising poverty and inequality across the country.

The Angel Project was an initiative to involve the community in the run-up to Christmas. Members at the chapel were asked to knit Angels (pattern provided) and then place them around the village for children to find, which was exciting for the youngsters as well as thought-provoking for the parents, with the Christmas Eve Service advertised as 'Angels and Carols' a place to re-unit the angels which had been found and hang them on the Christmas tree in the chapel.

As part of being active in the community some members volunteered to have Sunday morning coffee and chat sessions at the local cafés, but this was not entirely successful although Alan Measures continued the idea for a while, visiting the Post Office café and The Anglers.

In September 2015 the chapel began a course entitled 'Christianity Explored' which was an opportunity to consider 'the big questions of life' in the setting of a friendly house-group, one in an afternoon at Wendy Climer's house and an evening session at the home of Peter Walker. Whilst these sessions were well attended, providing an opportunity for current members to refresh and reflect on their own Christianity, there was little outside interest.

In the summer of 2017 Saxilby Methodists joined with St Botolph's to play their part in the new charity set up by the Duke and Duchess of Cambridge and Prince Harry, with the idea of getting people to talk, called 'It's OK to say'. Together the two churches planned meetings in a variety of places, where people could come and speak to someone in confidence.

Circuit services took place, giving opportunities for smaller congregations to come together and enjoy community worship, with uplifting singing and friendship.

If the weather was kind, members would take a picnic and spend time with people from other chapels.

Although there were few young people in the congregation, efforts continued to keep the chapel family in touch with the wider community. When Ingham Chapel closed in 2016, three of their active members came to Saxilby, taking the membership up to 48 for a time before it fell to 42 in 2017. For a time it felt things were looking up, with an ambitious building plan to remodel and upgrade the premises being explored.

Meanwhile the governance of Methodism was changing to keep in step with the needs and legislation of the modern world, requiring even the smallest chapels to put in place robust systems for issues such as safeguarding, security, safer recruitment and health & safety, and adding complex administration, unknown to previous generations. It was yet another difficulty to overcome, especially as plans for the building work had been shelved, despite hours of hard work from the Treasurer, David van den Bos, and Property Secretary, Keith Gerrish.

By 2019, Helen was now looking after so many other churches that she had less time to devote to Saxilby, which still had a membership of 34, but regrettably only about 20-25 people were attending services. The local leadership team worked hard to ensure fellowship continued within the smaller congregation, but the repair and maintenance challenges couldn't be ignored for long. When a major leak in the flat roof of the vestibule (the area that was built to access the school hall without getting wet) occurred in 2019, causing the chapel to be closed for a time and the congregation having to meet in the Village Hall (going back to its roots, so to speak), the future of the building became a major issue as structural concerns were identified that would be expensive to put right. On top of this, there was a significant shortfall in the amount of money coming in to pay the regular outgoings and Assessment, and with the chapel already running a sizeable deficit budget, no amount of fund-raising was going to be enough to carry out the necessary repairs and continue as before.

After a great deal of heart-searching and much debate, the Church Council finally acknowledged that Saxilby Methodist Church no longer had sufficient resources to maintain an active church. A meeting was held early in 2020 at which the sad and reluctant decision was taken to work towards closing the building at the end of August, but to manage this gradually, using the Chapel's 80th Anniversary in March to celebrate all the many achievements over the years, followed by a series of events to enable people from near and far to come and say goodbye to a much loved place of worship and fellowship.

Sadly the events planned to mark the closing couldn't take place due to the pandemic, so there was no opportunity to come together and remember the happy days before saying a final farewell, it was truly heartbreaking for the faithful congregation. Hopefully this book will provide some comfort by enabling people able to read the wonderful story of Methodism in Saxilby through the years. Readers can relive the remarkable history of the three different chapels, which had to adapt to change by uniting as one before moving onwards renewed and invigorated for another eighty years.

Even now, there is still a lasting legacy within the community, as I've discovered whilst writing this book, chatting with people and reading on social media about family connections with the chapel through christenings, marriages, funerals and Sunday School days. The chapel may have closed, but the foundations built over the years continue to leave their mark on the village today.

Saxilby Methodist Church just before it was sold

John Wesley began Methodism in small house groups, an idea which has been revived during the latter months of lockdown as regulations eased. This meant small groups of no more than six friends could meet together in each other's homes to watch services 'Zoomed' in from far and wide, sharing coffee and kinship.

As the cycle of change continues ever onwards we must explore ways of moving into the future. Maybe by going back to our radical roots, we can open our hearts and listen to the people who struggle to find relevance in religion today, finding ways to fulfil the challenge given by John Wesley all those years ago:

'Do all the good you can, by all the means you can, in all the ways you can, in all the places you can, at all the times you can, to all the people you can, as long as ever you can'.

KEY DATES

1808 Thomas Jackson brings Methodism to Saxilby

1808-1811 First Wesleyan Chapel built just off the High Street (lane still called 'Chapel Yard')

1839 **Wesleyan Centenary Chapel** opens further up the High Street (on the site of car sales) to accommodate the increasing congregation.

1849-51 **Wesley Reform Society** breaks away from the Wesleyans, initially using the old chapel of 1808, before building their own chapel on the High Street in 1851 (on the site now occupied by the Village Hall)

1852 **A Primitive Methodist Society** starts-up in the village, using the old chapel of 1808, recently vacated by the Reform Society.

1857 **The United Methodist Free Church** (referred to in the village as **The Frees)** is formed, incorporating many of the reform movements, including the Wesley Reform Society.

1875 The Primitives build a small chapel at the bottom of the High Street (on the site where the Fire Station stands)

1881 The Frees build a huge new chapel on their site on the High Street/Sykes Lane

1885 The Wesleyans carry out extensive renovations to their chapel at the top of the High Street, including building a new room for the Sunday School and a porch at the front

1888 The Primitives build a large extension to their small chapel, fronting on to the High Street.

1898 The Marriage Act allows non-conformist ministers to register marriages in chapels.

1932 Deed of Union signed at Royal Albert Hall, when the Wesleyans, the Primitives and the United Methodists (the Frees) finally come together. The united body to be known as **The Methodist Church of Great Britain**.

1937 The last service at the Free Chapel took place on 3rd January before the congregation amalgamated with the Wesleyans at the Centenary Chapel.

The UMFC Chapel is sold to the Parish Council for use as a Village Hall.

1940 **The Godfrey Memorial Methodist Church** opens on 21st March often referred to as the 'new chapel' home for the congregation from the 'Top Chapel' (the amalgamation of the ex-Frees and the ex-Wesleyans)

1944 The Primitive Chapel holds its last service on 3rd September and the congregation move to the new chapel.

Methodism in the village is once more united, almost 100 years after the three different denominations built their own chapels.

1946 The new chapel gets it's first resident minister, a tradition which carries on until closure. List of all Ministers and their families on separate page

1959 Sunday Night Hymn Singing is broadcast live from the chapel

2020 The Godfrey Memorial Methodist Church holds its last service on 22nd March, bringing to a close 210 years of Methodism in the village

BIBLIOGRAPHY

Barratt, George	*Recollections of Methodism & Methodists in the City of Lincoln (1866)*
Elvin, Laurence	*The Story of Some North Country Organ Builders (1986)*
Leary , William	*Lincolnshire Methodism (1988)*
Telford, John BA	*The Life of John Wesley (1886)*
Thornborow, Philip	*A Methodist in the Family (2014)*
Tomkins, Stephen	*John Wesley: A Biography (2003)*
Saxilby History Group	*Step Back in Time (2005)*
Selby, Wilfred E	*The Story of Wesley Chapel, Lincoln (One hundred years 1836-1936)*
Watmough, Abraham	*The History of Methodism in Neighbourhood & City of Lincoln (1829)*
Wearmouth, Robert	*Methodism and the Common People of the 18th Century (1882)*

REFERENCES

British Newspaper Archive

Lincolnshire Archives

Methodist Church of Great Britain

Methodist Heritage

My Methodist History

My Primitive Methodists

Oxford Centre for Methodism and Church History (OCMCH)

Saxilby History Group - *Special thanks to the John Wilson Photo Collection*

Wesley Historical Society

For information, the author may be contacted on hello@saxilbyhappydays.co.uk

ACKNOWLEDGEMENTS

Madeleine Ballard Scott, for the concept design of the front cover.

Christine Green for Dean Bemrose's collection of Saxilby memorabilia.

Chris Hewis, Chairman of Saxilby History Group, for agreeing to write the foreword.

Rev David Leese for his assistance in the planning stage.

Mick Saunders, for his support, as well as editing and proof reading the manuscript.

John Wilson for his dedication to preserving history by his collection of photos.

Recollections and memorabilia from members (past and present) of Saxilby Methodist Church.

LIST OF RESIDENT MINISTERS & FAMILIES AT GODFREY MEMORIAL METHODIST CHURCH

Rev. J. W. Lamb
1946-1948

Lodged in Saxilby, initially with Mr D Lang and family, then South Parade, before moving into the Manse

Rev. John Earl
1948-1952

Lived at the Manse, Homelea, Church Road, Saxilby with wife Kitty and daughter Leila

Rev. Bill Podmore
1952-1957

Lived at the Manse, Homelea, Church Road, Saxilby with wife Muriel and daughter Pamela

Rev. George Thompson
1957-1962

Lived at the Manse, Homelea, Saxilby with wife Betty and daughters Sheila, Pauline, Heather & baby Andrew Lindsey

Rev. Trevor Staniforth
1962-1968

Lived at Homelea, before moving into new Manse at 57 Mill Lane in 1966, wife Ena and children David & Rachel

Rev. Keith Handscomb
1968-1974

Lived at Manse with wife Pam and children Steven & Susan

Rev. Rodney Warden 1974-1978	Lived at Manse with wife Chris and children Andrew, Matthew, Daniel & Sam
Pastor Mark Powell 1978-1979	Lived at the Manse, 57 Mill Lane, Saxilby Came from Cliff College
Rev. Percy Allen 1979-1985	Lived at the Manse with wife Betty, *family had left home*
Rev. Ronald Todd 1985-1991	Lived at the Manse with wife Dorothy, *family had left home. Rev. Todd & Dorothy retired in Saxilby*
Rev. Lesley Whitehead 1991-1996	Lived at the Manse with husband Jerry and children Jamie & Katie
Rev. Tania Fowler 1996-1998	Lived at the Manse with husband Colin and daughters Emma & Rebecca
Rev. Nigel Hannah 1998-2003	Lived at the Manse with wife Eileen
Rev. Duncan MacBean 2003-2008	Lived at the Manse with wife Laura and children Shaun & Euan
Rev. Jo Lightowler 2008-2012	Lived at Manse with husband Andrew and boys Thomas & Matthew (both born at Saxilby)

Rev. Andy Burrows 2012-2014	Lived in Lincoln, overseeing Saxilby until new appointment made
Rev. Helen Hooley 2014-2020	Lived at Manse with husband David and children Jessica & Daniel

BV - #0050 - 090922 - C12 - 229/152/16 - PB - 9600198000106 - Gloss Lamination